All God's Chillun Got Worms

BY PEGGY VESELY

Printed in the United States of America.

First Printed in August, 2024

ISBN: 978-1-956544-63-3

Printed by Amazon.com

www.BetweenFriendsPublishing.com

Dedication

For Ed, the best cheerleader ever.

Contents

Prologue

There are many biographies out in the world. Mine is not a story of fame or fortune of heroes or tragedy. It is about a life lived with gusto, sorrow, and endurance.

I called it "All God's Chillun Got Worms" because I believe that everyone has bad times and good. Good relationships and awful ones. We learn and grow from the bad ones and appreciate the good ones more because we know that everything in life is not happy little cheerful stories.

I begin the tale with a history of the family stories I grew up with. I think they set the stage for who I am and where I came from and may explain a lot about how I handled my personal good and bad times.

I am proud of the person I became. I am not always proud of how I got here. But, because I truly believe everyone goes through these ups and downs, I have no sense of guilt about how I have lived my life. I hope you enjoy this tale of a simple life filled with worms.

Part I: Family History & Childhood

Chapter 1: The Beginning of the Saga

I want to tell you a little about the family tree that formed the base of who I am. My family's struggles began as their lives began. My early life was formed by my knowledge of these family struggles.

My mother was Ruth Evelyn Capell Barrett. She was born on May 5th, 1923, to Chester Britton Capell, who was born on April 8th, 1892. He was a handsome man who loved to preach, which is probably where I learned to love being on stage, but he spent most of his life struggling to earn a living. Her mother was Ethel Holcomb Capell, born in 1896. She was a woman who held grudges, yet loved me with all her heart.

My father was Robert Eugene Barrett, born May 16th, 1921. He was a man who loved deeply and wholly and truly lived a life of loving to make other people happy. Since his mother was not married at the time of his birth, he must have been called Robert Eugene Nickens at birth, however, by the time he went to school, he was known as Robert Eugene Barrett and I have never found any paperwork that showed him as a Nickens. His mother, Hattie Mae Nickens Barrett, born May 5th, 1902, in Atlanta, Georgia, was a tiny woman who lived a big life filled with chaos, but she always had a twinkle in her eyes.

These ancestors wrote the book on "All God's 'Chillun' got Worms." They led tempestuous lives filled with stories of missteps, kindnesses, and survival.

I probably knew my mother's parents best because I often spent a week or two with them in the summers as I was growing up. Grandma and Grandpa Capell always treated me special when I came to visit, and in later years when I felt totally alone, I always thought of them as two people who had always loved me.

Grandma Capell was born in South Georgia. She once took me to her mother's grave in a little weedy graveyard near Tifton, Georgia. She had seven siblings. Her mother died when Grandma was twenty-three. As the oldest child, she lovingly raised three of her siblings who were under ten years old at the time of her mother's death. I visited her sister, Delura, in South Carolina a few times as a child and I remember Delura loved Grandma dearly and often said that my grandmother was the only mother she ever remembered having and that grandma was always kind and loving.

This was the Grandma that made popsicles from Kool-Aid and sold them to the neighborhood kids for extra spending money. She always yelled to me when Grandaddy came in, "Is that Satan that just walked in the door?" She had caught him in bed with her sister many years before and never forgave him. The "worms" of that incident colored her life forever afterward. Divorce was unthinkable for them in those days, but punishment for sins was a truth they lived every day.

Grandpa Capell was a charmer. He loved to flirt and he loved sweets. He made the best pound cake I ever tasted. When I think of him, my earliest memory is a trip we made with him when I was about six or seven years old. He had some relatives that lived in Florida and we went to visit them. I am not exactly sure how he was related to them, but I heard somewhere as a child that he and his family were coming over from Scotland and all of his family died on the ship and that the people we visited were the family of a couple who were on the ship and adopted him. I have no idea if this story is true, but I loved it as a child. I found it to be so romantic! However, when I went to Scotland and saw the castle in Edinburgh, there was a group of people who would help you trace your ancestry and I asked them about Chester Capell. They were insulted and told me that Capell was not a Scottish name.

The legends we grow up with help shape who we are, and in hearing this story of sadness with a happy ending I grew up believing that you could make happy endings out of disasters. I knew that if something horrible happened to my parents, I might be adopted by a family who loved me. My childhood was filled with bad things, worms, happening to good people who survived and thrived

Mother liked to tell a couple of stories about her life during the Depression. Her father could not find steady work and went door to door offering to do chores for food and made sure he could take the food home to his family. Mother's older sister, Lillian, had told mother that it was shameful to let people know she was hungry and made her promise to never tell anyone she did not have anything to eat. So, when some ladies came to the school to make sure the children had something to eat, they asked each student to write down what they had for breakfast. Mother, following her sister's instructions, wrote down ice cream. When the ladies passed out the food, they did not give my mother any of the food. When she asked why they said they did not reward liars and she had lied on the sheet they had asked her to fill out.

Another time they brought shoes to the school for the children who had no shoes. A pair of black patent leather shoes fit her and she loved them so much she slept in them for weeks. The rest of her life she loved shoes. Some of the few arguments I ever heard her and my daddy have was about her spending too much money on shoes. After that argument, she would still buy more than one pair of shoes when they were on sale and hide them somewhere. Months later she would put on a pair of the secreted away treasures and daddy would ask if they were new. She would say, "Oh, no. I have had these quite a while." She would not lie directly to him, but she surely did not shy away from obfuscations. My parents' experiences in the Depression and their childhoods formed who they were. They were thrifty and worked hard to make sure we never went hungry or shoeless.

My father was fatherless and often shunned because he was a "bastard." He never told me any of the bad things that came of that condition. His stories about the Depression were about him and his grandfather gathering wild berries and fruits and drying them on the tin roof of a shed. They also knew where all the honeybee hives were and always had honey. My mother once told me that the reason she dated my father was that there were always pies available at his house. During the Depression there were no sweets at my mother's home, but the dried fruits, berries, and honey gathered by my father and his grandfather made sweets abundant at their house.

Of all of my family tree my father's story seems to be filled with the most "worms," but he was the happiest and kindest man I knew. It seemed that for him all of the "worms" made him appreciate the life he had more. He loved unfailingly and always woke me in the morning by saying, "rise and shine. Today is another beautiful day." It is amazing that I can still hear his voice and see his big smile when I wake in the morning and think of him.

Chapter 2: Peggy's Family Stories (Capell)

When telling the stories of mother's lack of food and shoes, I realized how the Depression hit the whole country. That townspeople felt the need to go to the schools and make certain the children had food and to donate shoes for them gives me a view of how everyone struggled in that dark time. It also made me realize how much it must have meant for my grandfather to get a job at a cotton mill where he was guaranteed a house to live in and food for the table. He happily took a job in Porterdale, Georgia, at Bibb Cotton Mill, where he worked and lived until he was sixty years old.

They lived at the very end of Spruce Street, which in my childhood was an idyllic place to visit. The street ended in a cul-de-sac and overlooked a railroad track. I could stand at the top of that hill and wave to the train conductors and they always waved back and sometimes tooted their big lonesome horns for me. On the other side of the tracks, some of the land was allocated to the workers at the mill to plant food crops. They grew corn, tomatoes, peas, beans, turnips, and collards. Past the food plots were wild blackberries and plum trees. When I picked the blackberries and plums, Grandma was always willing to cook me up a big juicy pie to brag about. "I picked these berries or plums," I would proudly say when offering pieces of pie around the table.

Beyond the berries was a river. I could sit on the bank and daydream and on hot days wade in the edges. One time one of the neighbor girls, Sara, and I took some potatoes from her house and dug a hole in the

9

bank of the river and built a fire and cooked the potatoes. Of course they were half raw, but we ate them with relish because we did it all by ourselves. These times with Grandma and Grandpa were at least every summer for two weeks from the time I was about seven until I was twelve.

Grandma loved plants and we often went to visit other people together. Our forays were often in search of new plants for her garden. She had friends all over the state of Georgia that swapped seeds and plant cuttings with her. She had broken her ankle when she was younger and walked with a cane, but that did not stop her from working in her flower garden every morning. I felt so important when she guided me on how to place the plant, and explained this plant needed full sun and this one liked a lot of shade. I wish I had paid more attention to the names of the plants. I believe she had a lot of exotic plants that I never see any more. Her dahlia plants grew taller than I was and the flowers sometimes exceeded the width of my hand. The colors were deep rich purples, bright brilliant yellows, and pinks and golds. My uncle, Henry Savage, built her a riser for the front porch that was covered with pots filled with plants she gathered from her friends in exchange for giving them cuttings and seeds from her store of plants.

She had a porch swing that was a gathering place at twilight. The adults sat on the swing or pulled out a chair from the house and we children played 'kick the can' until it got too dark, and then we would sit on the steps and listen to the adults until, totally contented we nodded off, only to be woken by the adults and put to bed when they finished talking. She had a vine strung across the front of the porch that provided shade and coolness on the hottest of those late June and early July Georgia hot summer days.

She had an apple tree that grew next to her kitchen window. She kept careful watch out that window to make sure the kids did not pick her apples. The apples were for pies and jams not for kids to throw at each other and waste. I often heard her yelling at the neighborhood kids to get away from her tree. One day I saw a beautiful red apple on that tree and thought Grandma was in another part of the house. In a blaze of daring, I decided that I was going to steal that apple, hide under the house, and eat it. I had almost reached it when I saw her standing at the window. I froze. She stood there a moment watching me, then she said "be careful. Get that pretty one and come on down out of that tree before you fall." For the rest of my life whenever I felt lonely, abandoned, or unloved, I recalled that moment when I knew I was very special to my Grandmother.

Chapter 3: Peggy's Family Stories (Lillian)

Mother wrote a story about Lillian, her oldest sister. I have copied it below.

January 15, 1997
My Beautiful Sister Lillian
My Sister and my Friend.

Since I was a young child she has had a very important role in my life. I can remember her as far back as living in Frog Alley in Quitman, Georgia. I suppose I was about five and she was about eleven. She taught me so many things. She took over for my mother about this age. I don't remember a lot about my mother. Especially when I was small or young. Lillian was always there. She was quite a girl. She fought for me, my brother Clarence, and my younger sister Lucy. Carolyn wasn't born then. She came into the family when I was nine and Lillian was fifteen.

I remember a lot of happenings in Quitman, Georgia. I don't remember what year it was, but my Daddy didn't have a job. Times were hard, but Lillian would never let anybody know we were poor. She had a pride that was unheard of.

We moved from Frog Alley where the frogs croaked to "Milltown." They called it this because we had a cotton mill there and most of the people worked there. We did pretty good until it shut down. And brother were we poor. But not my sister Lillian. She would tell me when I went to school not to tell anybody that I lived in Milltown. She would cut my hair, clean me up, and tell me to tell everybody I lived in town where rich people lived and I had a barber to fix my hair. I was not to tell what we had to eat. Make up something but don't tell them you didn't have any breakfast. So at dinner time the school let us go home for dinner. I would go home and come back but not to tell anyone I didn't eat.

One day this caught up with me. The teachers knew that some of the children didn't have sufficient food. So they came around in the rooms asking us to tell what we had for breakfast. I wrote down things that I thought rich people ate. Maybe ice cream and cake and a big peanut butter sandwich. I loved peanut butter to smell it. This little girl that brought her lunch to school had the most delicious looking sandwiches I had ever seen.

But this day I ran home and came back a little early and there was my friend that lived by me in Milltown eating the best looking food I have ever seen. We called her "Boots Bull." I asked her where she got that. She said they were giving food out to people they thought needed it. Of course I didn't get any. Well that one was hard to swallow. Because I sure was hungry.

But then one day somebody got suspicious of me and my tales. They said if you are so rich why don't you have any shoes? I probably stuck my head in the air and didn't answer that one – I'll go home and ask Lillian.

Back to my sister Lillian. She gave a boy a bloody nose with a brick for bothering my brother Clarence.

Well the great day came when we moved to Porterdale, Georgia, a long way from Quitman. My daddy got a job there and we moved. I'll never forget the real hanging electric lights. The lights hung from the ceiling so you could just reach up and turn it on. A far better light than we had with kerosene lamps.

My daddy wouldn't have to wash dishes for the town people any more for whatever they give him and my little sister, Carolyn, a baby at this time, would have some shoes. Someone asked Lillian, my sister, one day where the baby's shoes were or if she had any. She said "oh yes, she had left them in the house." I remember so well the day my sister Carolyn was born. We had possum and sweet potatoes. I couldn't eat it. I just couldn't.

In this new and beautiful house of four rooms I would get to sleep with my beautiful sister, Lillian. I don't know how she learned all she did. She was just born with pride. Pride to be clean. Pride to wash your hair. Octagon soap made her pretty black hair shine. We were all black -haired, but she had pretty white teeth and an olive complexion to go with her hair. She was a knock-out.

She soon went to work in the cotton mill. She taught me to wash my hair with Octagon and it would bring out the highlights. If you don't have a toothbrush, that is no excuse for not having pretty teeth. Get a clean cloth and some baking soda and brush away. When my sister was working in the mill she had to pass the school where I went to school. The boys would look out the window when they saw her coming and whistle. I looked to see who they were whistling at and it was my beautiful sister. One of the boys later married my sister, Carolyn. He was too young for Lillian.

I began to grow by leaps and bounds. I met a young man in school that wanted to date me. I was just fourteen. I told my sister about it and she said "He's cute, Ruth. Date him." His name was Gene Barrett. I later married him.

Lillian was visiting South Georgia. With some of my cousins. There she met Emory Willis. I don't know how long she dated him, but she married him and moved to Bridgeboro, Georgia. I had to adjust without her.

She and her husband lived there a short while and then they moved back to Porterdale where I could see her more often. They soon had a beautiful little girl and they named her Gloria. Lillian could make her some of the cutest clothes anybody had anywhere. She was always smart and very talented. She seemed to be able to do anything she set her mind to do. She would get little remnants of material and put them together and make beautiful dresses, underwear etc.

Lillian loves to cook. She is one of the best. She learned to make some of the best homemade biscuits in the South, when I was small. Probably not over nine. I watched her and learned to make them too. She would make them real small and neat. I picked that up from her and my husband Gene told me if I ever quit making those biscuits he would leave me.

Then Lillian and "Poss" as we called him had their second child. A boy, Kenneth. They loved those two children so very much. They soon purchased a store in Covington. It was first called The Economy Market.

Poss was a good business man and after several years he bought Russell Bradan's part and it became Emory Willis Market.

Now my beautiful sister had plenty of cuts of meat and she could really get down to her cooking. When you came to see her you sat down to the best eating in the country. T-bone steaks grilled outside. The works.

I'll cut this a little short, because I could go on and on but today I am fortunate enough to live within five or six miles from her and she bakes my husband and me pound cakes and food cooked in the wok. Brings it to us hot. She will say,

I just took this out of the oven or keep the wok till you eat it. It isn't as good after it gets cold. Or, Ruth will you and Sultan come over for dinner today? I just cooked some fresh turnip greens and corn bread or I'll bring it over if you want me to."

I'll not swap her so don't ask.

Happy Eightieth Birthday to My Beautiful Sister who encouraged me to write.

We love you, Lillian,

Ruth

Chapter 4: Gloria

As I grew older, I spent more time with my cousin Gloria, aunt Lillian's daughter. She was two years older than me and my idol. She was pretty and smart and her father had left the textile mill and opened a butcher shop. They moved to Covington and her life seemed much more exciting to me. She often was the cashier at the store and in the summertime, I was allowed to bag the groceries for her. Her father, Uncle Poss, sometimes gave me money at the end of the week for bagging the groceries. Gloria began to buy her clothes in Atlanta and I got her gorgeous hand me downs. I felt elegant and pretty in the clothes she passed down to me. The first house they lived in Covington was an old antebellum mansion just down the street from the butcher shop. It was huge and they only had furniture for a few rooms. Looking back, I also realize they probably didn't have enough money to heat the entire building. The kitchen was only connected to the house with a back porch. There were huge ballrooms downstairs and upstairs. What a wonderful place to daydream in, and I was a daydreamer. I constantly read fairy tale books and I dreamed of going to balls in long flowing gowns and dancing in those rooms.

That house was later torn down. When I see movies like "Gone With the Wind," I picture that house. As Poss and Lillian were moving up in the world, we were growing and prospering in Warner Robins. After WWII was over, daddy returned to Wellston Army Air Depot, later Robins Air Force Base, and got a job as an electrician on airplanes. He was so happy to be working on his beloved planes. We lived in the Zeigler Apartments, long rows of cement block buildings hurriedly thrown up for the growing population of workers coming to work at the new base.

When momma got pregnant with Robbie, she begged daddy to move somewhere less crowded. He found a farm house near Macon called Hook's Farm. My memories of living there include water that had to run a few minutes before the red rust changed to clear water, snakes in the seedy flower garden, and going hunting for rabbits with daddy. We set box traps with food inside and the rabbits were so cute when we found them there that daddy let me set them free. Having grown up with food that he shot and fruits that he found in the woods, I now think of how kind he was to me that he let me free perfectly good food. I got a dog, and wonder of wonders, I called her Lassie, as every part collie in the world was being named the same by all the little girls that had seen that wonderful movie.

For a while, daddy's friend, Walter Robinson, and his family moved into the other half of that crazy dilapidated farmhouse with us. They had a son who was a couple of years younger than me. He followed me everywhere and called me Paiggy. When daddy and I went to visit them a few years later on a farm in South Georgia, they had a dog named Paiggy.

While we lived on Hook's Farm, daddy bought an old, crashed Piper Cub airplane and set about repairing it. He took pilot lessons and once took me on a flight with him. We landed in a cornfield. He teased me and told me that he had deliberately faked the plane's engine shutting off. We flew out of there, so that may have been the truth. As a child I always accepted that story, but looking back, I realize he probably had some engine problem and told me it was on purpose so I wouldn't be afraid.

When winter came the old farmhouse was drafty and rats were in the walls. By spring we had moved back to Warner Robins into a duplex on Scott Circle. Robbie was born in June. I started school at Thomas Elementary in September.

Chapter 5: Daddy

From the moment daddy was conceived until the day she died there was a very special relationship between him and his mother. In 1920 when he was conceived, it was a disgrace to have a baby out of wedlock, and women were ostracized. Hattie was shipped to Alabama to live with an aunt who had no children and agreed to claim daddy as her own. Hattie hid her pregnancy from all around her for as long as she could, then, being the indomitable person she was, she fought back. She went back to Texas and bore a "bastard" with all of the awful consequences of doing so raining down on her head. After moving to Denver where no one knew her and getting altitude sickness, she decided to return to Georgia where everyone knew her and knew the child was fatherless.

The mill was glad to have a talented spinner back in their ranks, but the mill village had an area for good moral people and a separate one for those with less than high moral standings. Hattie, of course, was allotted a house on "the wrong side of the tracks." She thumbed her nose at her critics and went about her life. She met and married Mike Barrett and kept working at the mill. Mike was a lover, a gambler, and not always a good wage earner. She enjoyed the fun they had and tolerated the bad side of him. He was a charmer.

By the time daddy was eight or nine, he often came home to a house with no adults. He and his younger half sister, Helen, made do. They teased as siblings do and he said he often picked her up easily. Mike took daddy out and taught him to hunt rabbits and squirrels to supplement their meager funds for meat. Hattie loved to eat rabbit, squirrel, and frog legs. One of the things Mike stressed most to daddy was that you never took a loaded gun out of the woods. Therein lies the tragedy that met daddy. One day he came in from school and demanded that Helen get him some water. As sister's often do, she said, "You can't make me wait on you. Get it yourself." There was a rifle lying on the bed. Being absolutely certain that it was not loaded, daddy grabbed it, aimed it at Helen, and said, "I will shoot you if you don't do what I tell you." She laughed. He shot her. The gun was loaded. He said the shock was so great, seeing her leg bleeding, that he could not lift her. He ran to the street screaming," I shot my sister. I shot my sister. I shot my sister!" He was crying until a neighbor came and helped him get her to the hospital. Helen lost her leg. Daddy grieved for the rest of his life about causing her that hurt. She, on the other hand, denied he shot her and protested to anyone that would listen, "I was going to lie down and hit the gun and it went off." They truly loved each other.

Mike Barrett went after daddy with a baseball bat and daddy ran away and lived with an aunt for the next few years. I don't remember her name, I just remember her special love for daddy. Every time I saw her, she would tell me again about how hard he worked when he lived with them and what a big help he was to have around the house.

The boys in the mill village got up a baseball team and my uncles told me that my daddy was the best player on the team. The team began playing teams from other towns and winning and the little local papers began writing about the mill village team winning all the time, naming all the players and pointing out the best players. Some church ladies began following the team's games and realized that Gene Barrett was getting a lot of attention. They protested that the mill village should not be recognized to have a "bastard" leading their scoring, and made such a fuss that daddy was asked to leave. He made no fuss, just walked away. He never mentioned any of this to me in all of his stories about his childhood. The funny thing is, he never mentioned any of the stories about being mistreated. Those stories came to me from other people.

My favorite memories of him are his happy personality. Every morning he woke me with, "Rise and shine, Pennywinkle. Today is a beautiful day." With that beginning, the days were usually beautiful to me.

He is still here with me. When I am alone, he is there by my side telling me that this is a beautiful day. And most of the time it gets better when I hear him say that.

Chapter 6: The Rise of the Textile Mills in the South

Both the Barrett and the Capell family stories are inextricably tied to the cotton mills in Georgia and Texas. I googled "Post Texas textile mill history" and found an interesting thesis written on the rise of cotton mills in Texas. It is tied to the growth of cotton mills in the South. In 1790 at Pawtucket, Rhode Island, Samuel Slater developed a spinning frame and by the end of that year opened the first spinning mill in the United States. It was successful enough in supplying yarn to local weavers to merit expansion within three years, and within seven years the workforce expanded from nine children to over one hundred employees. In 1880 there was a Cotton Exposition in Atlanta that had as its central attraction a fully developed cotton mill with a Corliss Steam engine. Within eleven days a group of businessmen had bought this mill capable of running 10,000 spindles and a sufficient number of looms. This began the first and most powerful mill building surge in the South. The mills in New England largely used scrip as payment and built stores, schools, homes, churches, to make villages that totally supported their workers. The mills built in the South were very similar but generally paid meager wages in lieu of scrip. The workers were mainly women and children. From this, women became more independent and a different kind of women came to grow from this atmosphere.

I believe my grandmother Barrett, was very representative of this new kind of woman because she was a very skilled spinner. That meant she could work at any mill location. In my lifetime, I know she worked at Porterdale, Hogansville, and Jackson in Georgia, in Spartanburg, South Carolina, and in Post, Texas. When she became unhappy in any one place, she moved to another. She had so much freedom for a woman in the 1920s to 1960s.

She was born in Atlanta, Georgia, but in 1906, the businessmen at the mill her father worked at decided to invest in a mill being built in Post, Texas. They tried to get a manager to take a trainload of men to Texas and set up the mill that was built. None of the managers wanted any part of it. My great grandfather, Hattie's father, volunteered and was accepted for the job. So, my grandmother moved with her family to Post, Texas.

Which leads to a story that Grandma Barrett told me that I wasn't sure was fact. By my calculations, Grandma moved to Texas in approximately 1907. In 1916, Pancho Villa raided Columbus, New Mexico. When I looked at a map it looks like he would have come through Post, Texas, on his way to New Mexico. She told me that when she was about fourteen, Pancho Villa raided the part of Texas that they lived in and they had to run for their lives. She said they escaped in a wagon, but the wagon was full and she had to carry her baby brother.

I know that my father was born in Texas, and after he was born, Hattie went to Denver to work. She got altitude sickness and had to return to Texas. At some point thereafter, she returned to Porterdale, Georgia. By the time daddy was in third grade, he was working part-time at the mills and going to school half days.

Chapter 7: Sapharine

The times were hard times. The Depression left so many poor and the Civil War had wrecked the southern economy. Many of the stories of my father's life are sad, but, somehow, when he told them, they were just stories. Daddy had a sister named Sapharine. The only thing I know about Sapharine is that she dropped a nickel while out playing just at sunset and went in the house, got dressed for bed in her nightgown, and then decided to hunt for the nickel. She lit a candle and went outside. Daddy heard her screaming and saw her with her gown on fire running down the street. He chased her, knocked her to the ground, and tried to put the fire out with his hands. His hands were badly burned and Sapharine died. He used this story to warn all the children he ever knew about the dangers of playing with fire. Once, when my brother Robbie was about four, daddy caught him playing with matches under the house. He screamed and grabbed Robbie and held him to his chest, crying and yelling. That was the most upset I have ever seen my father and it served as a reminder the rest of our lives that playing with matches was dangerous.

My father had three other sisters: Helen, Daphne, and Mickey. Daphne and Mickey were younger than I was. It always gave Daphne pleasure to tell everyone she was my aunt when we were younger, but now that we are in our seventies, I don't think she likes for me to tell people that she is my aunt. Life is funny that way. My grandma Barrett visited me when she was in her seventies and I was in my thirties. She pulled me aside and asked if I was still using birth control. I assured her I was, but was curious why she asked. She replied, "Don't ever stop. God will fool you into thinking you are safe and then, whoops, there's another baby. He got me twice." I laughed and she smiled like she had given me the secret to eternal happiness. I loved her laugh and her sense of playfulness. She was feisty and smart and it was a joy to be with her.

Chapter 8: The Barretts and the Higginbothams

I remember sometime while Grandma Barrett lived in Hogansville going to a funeral for her sister who lived in LaGrange. I don't remember her sister's name, only that she had long black hair and long red fingernails. I was scared of her because I thought she was a witch, not because of anything she did, just because of the way she looked. And remember, I went to the movies every Saturday. This aunt was married to "Beno" Higginbotham. I don't know his real name, but that is the only name I remember. They had a son named Ralph. After WWII, Ralph and daddy went to work at the Air Force Base, then named Wellston Army Depot. All of my childhood was intertwined with Ralph and his family. Ralph's brother married my uncle Clarence's wife, Aunt Christine's, sister Dot. In my childhood, Ralph, his wife Faye, and Mom and Dad played cards together most every Saturday night. I remember falling asleep on their couch or ours listening to them giggle and tease each other. Their children, Bobby, Marilyn, Benny, Susan, and Jennifer, were the family that we knew and loved.

One summer after Beno's wife died, he and Claude Nickens, Grandma Barrrett's brother, spent the summer with us. Claude was my idol. He would go to the playground with us and demonstrate his agility on the monkey bars and parallel bars. You see, he was a tightrope walker with the circus and the circus was wintering in Macon, Georgia. What a glorious summer. Beno was an elephant trainer and Robbie and I got to feed the elephants and watch Uncle

Beno put the elephant through his paces.

While we are still at the Hogansville location, I have one more story to tell. I don't remember exactly how old I was but I have to admit to this criminal past, reluctantly. Daphne and I decided we would play in the back field behind their house. It was fall and we were hidden by the tall fluffy wild grasses that grew in that field. We decided we were camping out and we needed to cook us some food. This was before I knew about Sapharine. We snuck some matches from the house, pulled up some of the grasses, and started a fire. A breeze came up and the fire took off. We tried to put it out but it took off so fast we couldn't put it out. We ran to the house to tell someone, but when we looked back and saw the whole field being engulfed in the flames, we hid under the bed. In a little while, someone knocked on the door and asked who started the fire. The adults didn't know, and told them so. We never confessed until years later. The next day we saw where the woods had caught on fire and there was a dead cow still smoldering. I am not sure our parents believed us years later when we confessed to our crime, but the police never came after us. When I saw how angry daddy got at Robbie about playing with matches, I now wonder if some of that anger was not about his sister's death, but also about how his precious Pennywinkle could have been gone, too.

When I was little, I loved that he called me Pennywinkle. When I was about eight years old, I asked him what it meant. He told me that Pennywinkles were very active worms that were really good for fishing bait because they always moved enough to catch the eye of fish, and when I slept with my him and my mother when I was little, I moved around just like a Pennywinkle all night long. I wasn't sure I liked being called a worm, but as I grew older, I realized I loved having a pet name as it always gave me a warm feeling when he called me that.

Daddy's family liked nicknames. He was called Mary, though I never found out why. His sister, Helen, was called Boatin'. They both seemed to smile when one of the relatives used that name. Grandpa Barrett had a sister who lived in Macon. We called her Aunt Mae. She lived with a daughter and son-in-law who had a child named Melody. Aunt Mae always used Daddy's and Helen's nicknames when talking to them or about them. They both loved her dearly. She was what I think of as old south in her manners. When we ate at her house, she never sat down. She watched your plate, and if you ran out of anything she was right there with more. I remember taking my daughter, Colleene, there for dinner one time. I had taught her never to say she didn't like anything, just to leave it on her plate, or if she didn't hate it, eat it and make sure not to take any more. I don't remember what dish it was, but there was something that she took on her plate, didn't hate, so she forced herself to eat it. She almost cried when Aunt Mae dumped some more on her plate. Colleene looked at me like, "What do I do now?" I felt sorry for her and was proud that she was being polite and I said, "You don't have to clean your plate, honey. Save some room for dessert." I thought she was going to cry. She really did not ever want to eat at Aunt Mae's house again. Sometimes people can be too kind.

Chapter 9: Daddy, the War, and the Base

In 1944, World War II was needing more soldiers than ever before. For the first time the draft went out for married men with children. Daddy and mother's brother Clarence went together. They went to basic training at Fort Dix, then on a ship to Europe. When they loaded onto the ship all of the men were given shots for everything that they might face in the coming months. One of the shots was for malaria. Daddy came down with malaria and when they landed in France, he was shipped immediately to a hospital. The men in his group went straight to the battlefield. He told me he felt guilty that so many of the men he knew were killed in battle while he was in a hospital in France. Somehow, he felt they forgot that he was in the hospital until the people that were freed from the concentration camps started to need hospital care. He said visions of those emaciated people who were walking skeletons haunted him.

He was shipped to Austria to help clean up the towns that were captured but still had pockets of German soldiers hiding in buildings and woods. He once told me that he was so fascinated by how clean the Austrian women were. In the chaos and rubble of the war, they cleaned and swept the doorways and sidewalks that were near their homes, even if the sidewalks were broken and the doorways were tilted askew. He brought home a German rifle and some furs that he found in a box that could be made into a coat. Somehow, he and mama never found the money to get that coat made and eventually the furs started shedding and were thrown into the garbage. Georgia was too warm for fur coats anyway.

While he was in Europe, mama went back to Porterdale and got a job in the mill. We lived in an old hotel converted into apartments. Our kitchen and living room were on one side of the hall and our bedroom was on the other. The hall between the rooms was a general public hall and the bathroom was down the hall and used by all of the renters on the second floor. I loved standing on the balcony and looking out over the town and river. Since I was only four years old, I was forbidden to go there alone, but I often snuck out there anyway.

In 1946, daddy came home. I woke up in the kitchen on a pallet on the floor. I always slept with mama in the bedroom across the hall. I opened my eyes and there was daddy; my daddy was home. Joy flooded me as I ran into his arms and he hugged me so tight and cried.

He got his job back at the Army Air Base and we moved to Warner Robins. The story is that when he went to the base to get a job after the war, he told them that he had worked there in 1943. They told him that it was not a base then and there were no records of the men who worked there. He seemed so crestfallen that the personnel manager asked him where he got his mail if he worked there. Daddy told him there was an old hotel on Watson Boulevard that was a temporary post office for the workers. The manager laughed and said "Oh, yeah, you worked here then," and hired him and gave him credit for the two years he had worked there and his Army time. We loved being back in the fast-growing little town of Warner Robins. He built me a playhouse and I was happy and content. We moved to different houses, Hook's farm and Scott Circle. After we moved to Scott Circle, he and a friend, Jack Wiley, began to work part time at an auto repair shop in Macon. He would come in from the base, eat, take a nap, and go back to work. After about a year, the shop in Macon burned down and daddy and Jack bought a building from a base auction and a piece of rundown property and opened their own auto repair shop. The really nice thing about the building was that it was large enough to hold two cars being repaired and there was still room in the back for daddy to work on the airplane that he had bought.

I often spent Saturday mornings "helping" him rebuild that plane. He was very much a man of the time and did not let me use tools. "That was man's work." But I was allowed to help him brush on the finish on the airplane wings that was called doping the wings. Robbie was born in 1947 and mama was glad to have Saturday mornings to herself without worrying about me. I loved being with my daddy. Once the plane was rebuilt, he took me for rides in it. Then Mr. Wiley crashed it on takeoff by hitting a fence and we had to start all over again.

Daddy loved working on cars, not so much the engine parts, but he could get totally absorbed in taking out dents and getting the paint just right. He often made fun of cars that had "orange peel" painting. "Orange peel" was little, tiny bubbles on the surface of a paint job that, to daddy, showed a lack of attention to detail by the person doing the painting. To this day when I see those little bubbles on a paint job, I feel a sense of lack of pride by the painter. The funny thing is I sometimes see them on new cars on a showroom floor and no one else seems to notice them. One of his favorite jobs that he did for free was paint and repair the Masonic Lodge's clown cars. He had so much fun with thinking up wild and crazy paint jobs for those tiny little cars.

Keith was born in 1949, and as he and Robbie got older, they both learned to fix anything on a car and worked at the shop for extra cash and eventually repaired an old car for themselves. As I grew up, I went less and less to the "shop." When I was sixteen, my first car was a 1942 Ford that daddy had bought as Army surplus and painted and added plaid seat covers. I was so proud of that car and still feel a touch of nostalgia when I see one of those 1942 Fords in old movies.

Chapter 10: The Summer of 1949

Keith was born in May, Daphne and Mickey, my aunts who were seven and six years old, and my Aunt Carolyn, mother's sister who was seventeen, all came for the summer. We lived in a two- bedroom duplex. Robbie slept with me, while Daphne and Mickey slept in the other twin bed. Keith was in a crib in my parents' bedroom, and Carolyn slept on the couch. At the time, I just enjoyed having aunts younger than me that I could boss around, an aunt who worked in a drugstore at the soda fountain and made fabulous concoctions like cherry coke and ice cream cones with different flavors of ice cream, and the freedom to do anything I wanted because mother was so busy with everybody that she often lost track of where I was.

I realize now what a nightmare it must have been for mother. A newborn, three bickering girls, a toddler, and a teenage sister who was enjoying having no one supervise where she was all the time must have driven her crazy. What I know now was that Daphne and Mickey were only supposed to stay two weeks, but ended up staying two months. It is kind of blurry why that was, but I know mother was aggravated with daddy that he was not insisting that his mother come get the girls.

The girls and I made popsicles from Kool-Aid, (and a mess, I am sure) and we pretended to be doctors and nurses and raided the refrigerator at leisure. We played under the house on really hot days and I remember forcing my little aunts to taste my mud pie. Daphne and I fought. She bit and scratched, but I was bigger than she was, so when I got tired of fighting, I just sat on her until she gave up. On Saturdays mother dropped me, Daphne, and Mickey at the picture show on First Street. There was always a double feature, usually a cowboy movie (I loved Lash LaRue) or two, a serial such as Sky King, and a cartoon or two. That year there was a contest for the prettiest child and mother submitted a picture of Robbie. When they ran all of the pictures of the children, I was so proud to see my little brother's picture on the big screen. The cost of the movie was twelve cents. We each got a quarter: twelve cents for the show, five cents for a coke, five cents for a popcorn, and three cents left for penny candy. I always got Mary Janes because they came two to a package and the chewy caramel lasted a long time. We usually got there at noon and walked home around five o'clock. We felt so special being able to walk home all by ourselves and we were too tired to make any trouble. Until I started writing this, I always thought how kind it was of mother to take us to the show every Saturday. I now realize, it must have been the only sane time in her week for that whole summer.

Summer ended, and Daphne and Mickey went home. Carolyn went back to live with Grandma and Grandpa, and I got my bed back. Robbie slept in the other twin bed. It felt luxurious to have a bed all to myself again.

Chapter 11: Technological Advances in My Lifetime

As a child, in our home the entertainment of children was playing games outside, unless it was raining. Then there were board games such as Monopoly and card games such as war. I loved paper dolls and dolls. I remember especially loving to cut out the paper clothes and trying them on the dolls. The ones I made stories up for were families of dolls with little girls. Paper dolls often came as movie stars and I had one set that was Elizabeth Taylor and one that was Esther Williams. I loved the Esther Williams ones because she was an actress who always swam in her movies and the paper dolls had all kinds of bathing suits.,

Playing outside included games like 'kick the can,' hide and seek, 'mother may I,' and many others that we made up the rules on as we went along. We often played these games after supper while our parents sat on the porch and visited. We played until it got too dark to see. We also liked to catch lightening bugs and put them in jars to light up our play areas. We always had to release them before we went inside after quickly learning they did not survive in the jars overnight

Later the children lay on the floor as the parents sat around and turned on the radio and listened to shows like "The Lone Ranger," "The Shadow," and "Amos and Andy." Some of the shows were scary and some funny. We rarely listened to music on the radio since we had a record player for that. I remember dancing wild and crazy dances to those 78rpm records. I still sing "If I knew you were coming, I would have baked a cake," when unexpected guests arrive.

Television arrived at my uncle Poss' house several years before I knew anyone in Warner Robins that had a TV. Porterdale and Covington, Georgia, are much closer to Atlanta (about twenty miles) and early TV signals did not travel well to Warner Robins (about one hundred miles away). When I saw the first television show in Warner Robins, it was The Lone Ranger, and was barely visible for the "snow." The sound also faded in and out. In Warner Robins you had big outside antennas that the men would go outside and fiddle with trying to get a clearer signal.

By the time I was twelve years old, WMAZ had opened a station in Macon, Georgia, only twenty miles away and we watched only that station since it was the only clear one. Nearly everybody rushed out and bought a TV once there was a station near enough to get a reasonable signal. There was no such thing as remote control, but what did that matter, we only received one station clearly anyway.

I remember in the sixth grade each classroom had a TV on the day Dwight D. Eisenhower was sworn in as President of the United States. It was an historic occasion of the inauguration of a president being shown on TV. The televisions were only on loan for the day, we did not have TV in the classroom on a regular basis.

When I was in college, I had a business course that required us to write a program in BASIC for calculating how many supplies were needed per month for a manufacturing facility that made a product of our choosing. How very different is our usage of computers today! That type of information is now plugged into an app that calculates all of that for us.

My great-grandchildren are more computer savvy than I am. You would think that since I was there at the beginning, I would be better at it than they are, but as technology grew, I continued doing things by hand and felt more comfortable doing it that way, not making an effort to learn all of the new apps and upgrades unless I had to.

I like my smartphone with its camera, flashlight, voicemail, and texting. I love that I can keep in touch with family and friends on social media. I don't always like the arguments that erupt on these medias, but I do know more about the everyday lives of family and friends than I ever did when I depended on letter writing to keep up with people that were far away.

So, you can see I have gone through amazing times of changes in technology just in my lifetime. It is exciting to watch things change, but I try to hold on to old values I was taught in childhood: Be kind, love your neighbor as you would like to be loved, and don't tell bad things about other people that would hurt them. People don't have to think like you do to be good people, different people have different perspectives, so listen carefully because you may learn something.

Chapter 12: The Tornado

In April of 1953, when I was twelve years old, a tornado struck Warner Robins. I was in the sixth grade and had just gotten home from school and was changing clothes to go and babysit for a neighbor when I heard people screaming. I went to the front door and saw the lady across the street running down the street. There was a noise like a train coming and I looked to the west and saw a cloud shaped like a funnel winding like a snake and coming towards our house. I saw my mother at the door of the car next door and heard my neighbor say to my mother, "Ruth, you need to see to your children." I realized that the neighbor had his wife and children in the car and mother was trying to go with them.

As I stood there, mother dropped her hands and turned toward me. She looked ashamed. I knew her fear had overruled her sanity and I turned and saw the funnel cloud lift and turn toward the south so that it was not heading our way anymore.

Later that night all the women gathered on the porch of our neighbor, Mrs. Blount, and all the men left to go help search for survivors. I was supposed to be babysitting for Mrs. Blount. She had six children. The oldest was my age, but he was a boy and everybody knew boys did not take care of babies well. Her daughter, Linda, was two years younger than me and told everyone that when she saw everyone running, she picked up the baby and ran across a field going the same way as everyone else. However, when she looked down and saw some wild strawberries in the field, she sat down with the baby and ate strawberries.

The men were gone most of the night, when they came home in

the early morning, the women fed them and we all went to bed. A few days later we went riding around the area that had been hit and one image stays in my mind: The whole building had been swept clean by the tornado, but on the bare foundation stood a china cabinet with one cup still hanging from a hook. There were pictures in the paper of bears in a tree, a car on a telephone post, and whole areas of piles of cars and wood and junk. For years afterwards, people dug storm shelters, and watched the darkened skies of storms with fear and trepidation.

The other story that sticks in my mind is daddy and the men talking about the Red Cross. The Red Cross had sent trucks around the town asking for donations of clothes and canned food for the people who had lost their home and everything they owned. People had given generously and the City Hall was stacked with the bountiful donations. The Red Cross set up a table to pass out the donations to the people in need, but they required each person that took a donation to sign a statement saying they would pay it back when they got back on their feet. The Mayor saw this and gathered some men together and ran the Red Cross out of town and the churches provided workers to distribute the donations with no strings attached. It was a long time before the Red Cross had any supporters in Warner Robins again.

Warner Robins was the first to be declared a Federal Disaster Area. People helped each other and we slowly recovered. Other things took over and normal life returned.

Chapter 13: Early Childhood Lessons

I was really scared on my very first day of school. Mother dropped me off at the front door and drove away. When I went in, I did not know where I was supposed to go. I noticed everyone looking at lists on the doorjambs, but since I couldn't read, I didn't know what they were looking at. Mrs. Brantley, the school principal, saw me standing there in the hall almost in tears and asked me where my mother was. I told her my mother dropped me off at the door and left. She looked at me kind of funny, then took my hand and said, "Well, let's find your classroom." She started down the hall with me in tow and read each one of the doorjambs to me until she read Peggy Barrett. "That's me!" I cried. She smiled at me and introduced me to my teacher. When I look back on that day I realize what a kindness it was that she read the names to me without asking for my name. It took her longer, but I learned what the lists on the doors were about and how I needed to learn to recognize my own name when written down.

I had never been read to as a small child, and when I discovered books, I was enraptured by the worlds you could escape to. I loved Dick and Jane and their cat and dog and their mother and father. I had one little problem though, I loved to talk and I talked really loudly. In the back of my first grade classroom there was a coat closet with slatted doors. I found there was room for a desk in that closet. I could hear all of what the teacher said, but I could not see anyone to talk to. I spent a lot of time in that closet. The funny thing is I knew it was fair, for I needed to learn to control my talking. At one time, I started talking to the teacher in the middle of one of her lessons from the closet and she put me in the hall outside the classroom. Mrs. Brantley, the principal, found me sitting in the hall. "Oh, Miss Peggy, what have you been up to?" I told her that I talked too much. She smiled and took me into her office and explained to me very kindly how important it was to be quiet in the classroom when the teacher was talking. I felt special and I would like to say I improved my outbursts of talking, though I still spent a lot of time in the closet for the rest of the year.

In second grade the class was divided into three reading groups by ability. We read out loud each day and as a pupil improved, they were moved up to the next reading group. Some of the children already knew how to read when they started school, so they were immediately in the first reading group. I struggled with reading, having only learned my alphabet and very basic reading skills in the first grade, so I began in the bottom reading group. My love of reading soon helped make a big improvement in my skills, and within six weeks I was advanced to the middle reading group. Everything was really going well until I made a big mistake. I lied to my teacher. She had announced that on each child's birthday they would be allowed to leave the room to go to get some water or to go to the bathroom without asking for the whole day of their birthday. After a couple of the kids in the class had basked in this privilege, I wanted very badly to have a day like that. I asked the teacher what about the kids with summer birthdays and she said that it was only on the actual day of your birthday that you had that privilege. I thought about that and decided that I was being robbed since my birthday is July 5th. So I determined to tell her it was my birthday on a school day. So, one day I announced that it was my birthday. She allowed me all of the privileges of the birthday kids, but after that I felt she disliked me. What I realize now is that she had my birthday written in her attendance book and knew immediately that I was making up a birthday so I could get the special day treatment. She never called me on it, but I never made the first reading group. I decided that I probably deserved that and determined that telling lies was not the kind of person I wanted to be. I really liked it better when she liked me, and having a day of being special is not nearly worth spending the rest of the year shamed for having done something wrong.

Life has so many little lessons that teach us how to treat each other. I gradually learned to talk less in class and to lower my voice when necessary. However, my loud voice really paid off when I decided to do some acting in community theater. It is amazing how many parts you get in plays in some part because your voice carries beautifully throughout the theater.

I continued to love learning for the rest of my life and I attribute that in some part to the sweet feeling of safety that my dear Mrs. Brantley gave me in first grade.

Chapter 14: 3-5th Grade

By the third grade I had learned to talk quieter in class, not to interrupt the teacher, and to be more careful with the truth. My reading ability had grown by leaps and bounds and I was a really good student. Amazingly enough I became teacher's pet. I was allowed privileges other students were not allowed. If another student was absent, I could sit in their seat for the day. No one else in the class was allowed this privilege. Along with this amazing freedom came a life's lesson. When we finished a test and went outside to play everyone talked about what they didn't know or weren't sure about on the test. At first, I just told everybody, "Oh, that was an easy test. I think I made a 100%." I began to notice that I wasn't so popular with the kids who had been my friend in the second grade and that I was the only one who bragged about knowing all the answers. Oops! I began to think hard about the tests and there was always at least one question that was harder to figure out than the other questions. When discussions about the test took place, I answered honestly that I had a hard time with that question. Attitudes changed back and I became a part of the games on the playground again. That was a lesson that has stood me in good stead for the rest of my life. When people have problems in life, I always try to understand what their problems are and put myself in their shoes. Responding that way to others problems makes life more interesting and creates bonds of friendship that last throughout life.

By fourth grade, my third grade teacher, Mrs. Cox, had spoiled me rotten. I felt I deserved to be treated best by the teacher. My fourth grade teacher did not feel the same. The schools in Warner

Robins had become overcrowded with the influx of new jobs and new families to the base. The powers that be decided to put two of the fourth grade classrooms in a building that was previously used as a recreation area for local employees of the base. It had two large rooms and bathrooms. It was a couple of blocks from C. B. Watson School. That meant that the teachers didn't have to worry about the principal dropping in unannounced. My fourth grade teacher loved to have her hair combed and if you combed her hair you could avoid some of the class assignments. I liked avoiding assignments as much as the next pupil, but I did not want to brush or comb her hair. When I refused this privilege a couple of times, I noticed a decided chill in her attitude towards me. But, since I was still cocky about my mental abilities, a gift from Mrs. Cox, my third grade teacher, I raised my hand to answer every question my new teacher, Mrs. Johnson, put to the classroom. I think she resented the fact that I was rarely wrong. Once, while I was out sick, she taught multiplication by zero. On the day I returned to class we had a "math bee." This was where everyone in the class stood in the front of the classroom together and the teacher called out math problems. If you missed the problem, you sat down. If you got it right after someone else missed it, you stayed standing. I was usually the last one standing. On this day I was second in line and she asked me what four multiplied by zero was. I had missed the lesson the day before and figured that if you had a four and multiplied it by nothing it would still be four. I missed it and had to sit down. I was devastated. She said, "So, miss smarty pants, you don't know everything, do you?" The rest of the class kind of nervously giggled. The strange thing was that after that, the rest of the class was kinder to me. I think even at the age of ten children realize that nobody should treat anyone else unfairly, and many of them no longer liked her so much.

In fifth grade the powers that be had miscalculated as to how many students they would have. On the first day of class, they came to each fifth grade classroom and asked if there were any volunteers to go to another classroom at the other building that would be taught by Mrs. Johnson. Many of her former students from the year before quickly volunteered. They liked her and they liked the freedom at the other building where we went outside to play more often than the big school did. I kept my head down and did not volunteer. My new teacher, Mrs. Meecham, had a northern accent. I had never heard anyone talk like that before and even though I didn't always catch every word she said, I was fascinated by her voice and pronunciations. She read to us each day after lunch and encouraged us to take a nap. I remember one story that she read. It was written as though the speaker was a hen and the human was "the hand." It fascinated me by putting me in the mind of someone that was afraid of a hand.

We had spelling tests each Friday and got a gold star if we got all of the words right. I prided myself on those gold stars. One week one of the words was "vase." Being a southerner, that was pronounced slightly different than the way my teacher said "vas." I had no idea what that was. I wrote "was." I missed getting a gold star for that week, the only week in the whole year. Isn't it funny how something so simple sticks in your mind for seventy years and so many other things slip away?

Like so many children, I was busy finding my way and my place in the universe. I liked being the best at something, even something so minor as spelling tests. I was not very athletic. I wasn't the most popular. I wasn't the prettiest or the kindest, but I was the best speller in the class. I think we all strive to be the best at something, and as time goes by, the class size we are competing with gets larger. As an adult, I learned to compete against myself instead of other people. If I could just type better today than yesterday, or paint a painting better than before, or find a book that I liked better than the one I had just finished. For me, that makes life easier. I pride myself on my accomplishments, but they are not diminished by the fact that other people do them better than I do and I do not look at other people as competitors for my place in the hierarchy. Everyone had strong points and weak points. I am not better than anyone or worse than anyone. I may do some things better than you do but you have strengths that I cannot hope to attain. It levels the playing field and keeps me from being the "smarty pants" that my fourth grade teacher so disliked.

Chapter 15: 6th and 7th Grades

When I was going into the sixth grade, Warner Robins had grown enough to support another elementary school. Westside School was built and I began the sixth grade in a brand new school. It was closer to home, only three blocks from our house. I loved my new school and my new teacher, Mrs. Hannah. After roll call each morning, she let a student entertain us or we sang. We had one boy in the class, Sanford Chatham, who sang beautiful cowboy songs, and Sylvia Teal who was taking voice lessons and sang operatic songs. When they didn't sing, we all sang a few old songs in rounds. We also sang patriotic songs like "America the Beautiful." It always started the day off on a happy note.

I was still a talker, but Mrs. Hannah was a very wise teacher. Our new school had a library all its own. When I finished a lesson and began to talk to another student who was not through with theirs, Mrs. Hannah would send me to the library. What a wonderful place! New books I had not read awaited me there. There was a series of biographies that I fell in love with. I learned about Abraham Lincoln, Amelia Earhart, Benjamin Franklin, and on and on. By the end of that year, I had completed the whole series of twelve biographies. We had a playground with swings and monkey bars and a merry-go-round. The only sports equipment we had was a baseball field and softballs and bats. I was a terrible ball player. I was always selected last when the captains of the teams were picking players. I always hit the ball straight to first base, so we were guaranteed an out each time I came up to bat. I never improved in sports very much, but I was always enthusiastic. We had a male science teacher, Mr. Smith, who was also our Physical Education teacher. When the first report cards came out that year, I was so unhappy to see I had made all A's, except for Physical Education. I went to Mr. Smith crying. I showed him my report card with all the A's and reminded him that he kept telling us that it was not important if we were good at the sport, the only thing that mattered was if we tried hard and were good sports. Between my tears and my calling him on his profession that it didn't matter if we were good, he changed my grade to an A and continued to give me A's the rest of the year. After all, no one could claim that I didn't try my best.

Seventh grade was great. My teacher, Mrs. Gould, was strict and an excellent teacher. When I finished a lesson quickly and turned to talk to another student, she would put me to work. I cleaned blackboards and dusted out erasers. That sounds like a punishment, but I was so proud that she trusted me to go outside and dust the erasers and clean her blackboards better than anybody. I enjoyed every minute of those tasks and did not bother any of the other students. The elementary schools at that time in Warner Robins were first through seventh grade, so we were graduating from seventh grade to go to the local high school. We even had a seventh grade prom. In preparation for the prom, we had dancing lessons in the cafeteria two afternoons a week for an hour each. We learned how to square dance. I had started noticing boys a little in the sixth grade, but we were having dates to the seventh grade prom, so all the girls and boys were watching each other and interacting more in that kind of ritual where you decide who you would like to go to the prom with. Some of the girls bragged about getting multiple offers and how hard it was to decide who to go with. I only got one invitation from Donald Wooley. I liked Donald, but wished I was more popular and had more offers to brag about. On the night of the prom, I had a beautiful prom dress and he brought me a corsage of beautiful carnations to pin on it. My mother was so proud. We danced, drank some Kool-Aid, had some cookies, and went outside to sit on the swings to cool off. Donald said he had something to confess to me. I froze. What could he be talking about? He said that a couple of the other boys had planned to ask me to the prom, but he had told them that he would beat them up if they asked me, "cause he was taking me to the prom no matter what." I laughed and hugged him and felt better. Our little affection for each other lasts to this day. Occasionally I still see him around town and always feel that affection.

About halfway through the seventh grade I began to really like math. I loved solving the problems and became very quick at it. Mrs. Gould decided that another tact instead of washing blackboards was a better road for me to travel and began to introduce me to algebra, and I loved it.

Chapter 16: Ed's Favorites

When I write these stories, I read them to Ed. He edits, critiques, and suggests other stories that I have told him over the years. Recently he reminded me of a story that I always get a laugh about regarding my time in first grade.

As I told you before, I had a real problem with talking too much and too loudly in first grade. We had desks, but sometimes we sat at tables with five other students. One day I was sitting across from Pam Crosby, my best friend in first grade. We had been talking, with me trying especially hard to be quieter, Pam got louder as she talked to me. The teacher said "Peggy, I have told you before not to talk in class." I protested that it was not me this time, it was Pam. Pam lived right across the street from the teacher and the teacher really liked her. "I know Pam," she said, "and it was not her." So, I was sent to the closet. Well, Pam became an operating room nurse, and when I was in my late twenties I was having a procedure in the hospital where Pam worked. They had given me a shot to relax me before taking me into the operating room. When I saw Pam, I said "Oh, Pam, why didn't you tell Mrs. Johnson that it was you that was talking and not me in first grade." When I woke up, I apologized profusely and Pam and all of the nurses laughed and laughed and said, "You would be surprised what comes out of people's mouths when they have had that shot." I cannot believe that I had remembered that for all of those years.

The next story is from eighth grade. My math teacher on the first day of class was explaining that we were going into a new phase of learning in math: algebra. She said, "I know none of you has ever seen anything like this" and wrote 2X=10 - 4 on the board.

"I have," I said. She turned to me and said "Okay, come show the class how to solve it."

I solved it, which made her angry. You remember Mrs. Gould in the seventh grade was giving me algebra problems to keep me busy when the other kids were occupied with their studies and she didn't want me to disturb them. I still had not learned to keep my mouth shut. My math teacher was rude to me the rest of the year. If I ever asked a question, she would say I was a smart kid I should be able to figure that out for myself. The funny thing was that by mistreating me, she alienated the rest of the class and they played tricks on her. One mean trick that I would never have condoned if they had asked me was really awful. The football team used our classroom for their locker room. One morning after a football game the night before, the teacher smelled something in the back of the room and went back to investigate. There were some coffee cans on the shelf above the coat racks. She pulled down one of the cans, kind of tilting it toward her to see what was in it. It spilled all down her dress. The boys had defecated and urinated in the can and left it for her. She went home. I adjusted to her and just never asked questions in her class. I didn't like her, but in life we adapt or become unhappy. I was never an unhappy child. Some people were just nicer than others and I just learned to ignore the ones who were not as nice. She was fair in her grading and I made my A's in her class and loved algebra.

The eighth grade classrooms were in the school that was called Warner Robins High School. However, as Warner Robins continued to grow, the town built another high school. The new high school was ninth through twelfth grades, so we were the youngest class two years in a row. The new high school became Warner Robins High School and the old one became Warner Robins Junior High School.

In eighth grade I went to the county spelling bee as one of the two best spellers in Warner Robins. I missed the word "accelerate." I spelled it "axcelerate." It was my last foray in big time spelling, but I do love crossword puzzles and Scrabble games to this day.

Part II: First Love & It's Ending

Chapter 17: The Church of God

I have always loved going to church. I loved the stories and the companionship of the children that I met there. I remember going to Vacation Bible School in Porterdale at the Porterdale Baptist Church when I was visiting Grandma Capell for my two weeks in the summer. The teacher was kind and we had snacks, listened to stories from the Bible, and drew and colored pictures. What is not to like about that? I remember the teacher telling us to be careful what we pray for and always make sure to say at the end, "Not my will, but thine, O Lord." I believe in my very being that as humans we are often tempted to change plans that God has because the road he has planned for us is not always easy. We grow through the trials we face. I tell my stories about my trials as I hope always to give comfort to others as they experience trials in their life. A trial is somewhat easier when you know something similar happened to someone else and they not only survived it but found happiness afterward.

Most of my friends went to the Baptist church and I attended with them and enjoyed it. When I was in the fourth grade, I asked my mother to go to church with me. She said she would go with me if I would go to the Church of God, a Pentecostal denomination in our town. I began to go to the Church of God and went for several months before she began to go with me. I did not understand some of the rituals at the new church. They sang louder than the Baptist church and sometimes people would begin singing and praying really loudly and then they would break into "speaking in tongues." The church people explained this to me as the spirit of the Lord moving these people and speaking through them. This was considered a sign that God has chosen you as a special person. I wanted to be a special person so I began to go to the altar every time they called for people who wanted the Holy Spirit to come and pray. And one night, I began to speak in tongues. I was so happy. I knew for sure God loved me and found me to be special.

If you had the Holy Spirit, there were a lot of things that you had to do differently to show the world that you were no longer part of the world but part of a chosen people. You had to do all the stuff they taught you at the Baptist church like tell the truth, be kind, not drink alcohol, and never cuss. But, to show you were filled with the Holy Spirit you also had to quit going to picture shows, never wear shorts, don't cut your hair, don't wear makeup, don't dance, and many other things.

I went to my seventh grade prom and danced because I discussed it with my preacher and he said square dancing was different because you only touched the boy's hand when you square danced. But by the time I got to eighth grade, my friends were going to dances and movies with groups that included boys and it would be a sin if I went with them. Also, since I couldn't wear shorts, I was excluded from all sports. When the rest of the class went to Physical Education class, I sat on a bench and read. It was isolating. My only friends became children that went to the Church of God and I didn't get along with them as well as my other friends. I don't think they liked me very much. They would play tricks on me. Once they came to me and said they really would like to have a wiener roast but their parents wouldn't let them have it at their houses, so would I ask my parents could we have it at our house? I got really excited and my father dug a fire pit in our back yard for the cookout. On the night of the party no one showed up except a boy I had a crush on. I called several of the girls and they laughed and said they had to wash their hair. I felt totally alone and I just knew the boy thought I had set it up to get him alone. He was kind and polite but left as soon as I found out no one else was coming. I distanced myself from them somewhat but still only had them as a group to go places with because they didn't dance or go to movies either. We met at their houses and played games or just laughed and talked. Sometimes we went to drive-in restaurants, met boys, and had hamburgers.

One night we met several airmen from the base and told them that if they wanted to see us again, they had to come to our church and meet our parents. Surprise, surprise, four of them showed up the next Sunday. After church we all went over to the Jones' house and laughed and talked. The next night all of the guys showed up at the Jones'. I wasn't invited. The guys paired up with the girls that were there. One of the guys, Frank Riley, called me while they were there and asked me to come over, but I lived across town and had no way of getting there. The next day at school, I asked them about Frank and they all laughed and said he had "made out" with Sheryl Miolen and they were dating now. I again felt left out, but they all lived near each other and close to the base, so that made sense to me.

About two weeks later, Sheryl came to school crying because her father had forbidden her to date an airman any more. He said she was too young at fifteen to be seeing an airman. That evening Frank called me and asked could I come over. I said I didn't have a ride. He said one of the guys had a car and they would come get me. Mother agreed. Thus at fifteen I began dating my first husband, Frank Riley. He was charming, good looking, and I felt like I belonged.

Chapter 18: Courtship

I was so thrilled to be dating Frank. He was charming, handsome, and my first kiss was all I had dreamed about. He was gentle, and by the time he kissed me, I believed that all of the love stories I had ever read had come true. I felt that kiss from the top of my head to the bottom of my toes. I had read how exciting a kiss was and it was all of that and more.

We dated sitting on the couch and talking, taking walks, visiting with my friends, and sometimes double-dating with some of the airmen he knew. He was jealous if I talked too much to these airmen, but that was exhilarating. He wanted to keep me for himself. I had no experience to check any of this by. I quickly decided I was "IN LOVE." He proclaimed his love for me especially when he was pushing me a little farther into the petting stage. I willingly followed. It was like being on a mountain top. The air was thin and I gasped for breath, but I willingly followed every step of his sweet seduction. We spent a lot of time alone in the woods or in the living room while mother and my brothers watched TV in the other room. I was forbidden to go to movies, dances, or other places with no supervision and no one else interfering. I prayed to God to give me strength to resist that last pressure to "go all the way." The prayers did not help. I succumbed and loved it. There was no going back. Two weeks before my sixteenth birthday, the facts were indisputable: I was going to have a baby. It took the next two weeks to work out a plan. Georgia law required that a girl be sixteen to be married with parental consent. It required that a man be twenty-one or have parental consent. Frank wrote his parents and got a letter of consent. On my sixteenth birthday I broke the news to my parents: Frank and I were getting married and I was having a baby.

It amazes me looking back how different my parents' reactions were. My father was furious with Frank and my mother was ashamed of me. Mother cried and cried about how she thought I was a "good girl." How could I do this to her? My father said, "You don't have to marry him. We can fix this." I faced my father and told him that I loved Frank and this was what I wanted to do. I am not sure that was the truth. I had so many plans about college and being the first woman to go to Georgia Tech and becoming an engineer and all of those plans had to be shuttled. I had sinned and I needed to pay the price. Another part of me was excited about being on my own and having a life with this handsome charming man who was to be my husband. I put aside the nagging doubts about his having informed me that he was liable to be charged with statutory rape if he didn't marry me. Looking back, I realize it was a real part of his decision to marry me. We were so young and so starry eyed we were both sure that this was truly LOVE.

My birthday was on the fifth of July and the wedding was in my front yard on eight days later in 1957. Mother and daddy left to go to Texas to visit Grandma Barrett that afternoon. Frank and I had our wedding night in their bed. I woke up at two o'clock that morning to Frank wandering around the house. When I asked him what he was looking for, he said, "where is the pail? I need to mop the floor." I realized he was sleep walking. I shook him. He woke up, looked around and said, "What am I doing in the kitchen." I told him that he was sleep walking. He nodded, climbed back in bed, and immediately was back asleep. I lay there in amazement at this phenomenon. I had never seen anyone sleepwalk before.

The next day, we got on a bus and headed to Kentucky to see his family.

Chapter 19: Kentucky & Cincinnati

I had never been outside the South. Florida, South Carolina, and North Carolina were far away to me. The bus ride to Kentucky seemed to take forever, but we went through mountains and the scenery was beautiful. The people on the bus were friendly and it was exciting. I got carsick and a doctor on the bus got the soda fountain guy to fix me a drink with just the Coke syrup. It settled my stomach immediately. Everyone kept asking me was I okay and in my natural tendency to talk, I told them all that I was a newlywed and on my way to meet my in-laws. Everyone joined in to tell me how kind people from Kentucky were and how they were sure my in-laws would love me.

The Riley clan was a shock. When we got to the house in Verona, Kentucky, Frank and his mom immediately went in another room and shut the door and left me sitting on the couch alone. Frank had three brothers and one sister still living at home. One brother, Herbert, was married and in the Air Force, stationed in Florida. None of his family said a word to me as they just walked through the room checking me out. I was amazed when the phone rang and I saw the phone on the wall. It was a wooden box with a crank and a mouthpiece on a cord, just like in the old movies.

When his mother, Elsie, came out she demanded that I give her my purse. I hesitantly handed it to her, appalled. She said she would hide it so that her youngest boy Randy wouldn't steal all my money. Randy was five years old. I couldn't believe that the answer to him stealing was to hide the purse, but I gave it to her and she walked out of the room. Frank just shrugged his shoulders and called all the family in to introduce me. The boys were Vernon (fifteen), Booby (twelve), Randy (five), and his sister, Susan, who was eight years old.

We had dinner and went and sat on the front porch until dark. People drove by and honked their horns, waving at us. We went to bed at dark in a bed that had a spring coming through a hole right in the center. I was fascinated by this whole experience and very intimidated. But everyone was friendly enough, and in the morning we visited a while then went to the bus station and caught a bus to Cincinnati. Frank could not wait for me to meet his friends. His family had lived in Cincinnati when he enlisted in the Air Force and he didn't know anyone in Verona.

Frank always claimed that he headed a gang in Cincinnati and they had robbed a jewelry store when he was seventeen. The youngest gang member was thirteen and got scared and turned the jewelry into the police. Because Frank was almost eighteen and they didn't have really hard evidence that he had planned the robbery, he was given the opportunity of joining the Air Force instead of going to jail. He took the Air Force. I don't know if that was truth or braggadocio, but the friends he introduced me to were very happy to see him and treated him with the respect you would expect from a leader of a group. We walked by a photo studio and Frank went in to talk to the manager. The manager asked could he take a picture of me to display in the window. I was flattered and I think it pleased Frank. The next time we visited Cincinnati there was my picture in the studio window. I felt beautiful. When his friends turned their attention to me, however, he was not happy. He was always very jealous of any attention I got. I thought it was love and was thrilled. When I got too much attention, we got on the bus and went back to Verona earlier than we had planned.

On Sunday, his mother asked if I wanted to go to church with her, but Frank declined for me. After they left, he told me that they handled venomous snakes as part of the service and he didn't want me to be exposed to that. I had heard about that kind of service through some of the revivalist preachers that had come through the Church of God, but had never actually experienced it and really did not want to try it.

The next day his mom took us to see his grandfather. In order to get to his grandfather's house, you drove off the highway onto a dirt road for several miles, then you parked on a little side road, walked down a valley, and then up the side of a mountain. They lived in a little log cabin overlooking the most beautiful scenery. They had no running water and no electricity. The grandfather was in his eighties and on his third wife. He had outlived the others. His wife told me a fascinating story. When she first came to live in the cabin with him, every day at sunset the rocker on the front porch would begin rocking. When she asked what made the rocker rock, he told her that his wife who had died visited every day at sunset and that is where she sat, just like she had all of her life. When the new wife insisted he put the rocker on the back porch, it still rocked at sunset. Finally, she insisted that he burn the rocker, so he did. Now the front porch in the place where the rocker used to sit still creaked each day at sunset. She said she just had to learn to get used to being watched over by his long gone wife.

I asked Frank's mother how she had met Gran, his father. She hesitated a long time and Frank told her to tell me that it was a good story. "Well," she said looking down, "I don't know if it is romantic or horrible but here it is. My sisters and I were at a barn dance and these three young men rode in on horses, pulled out guns and picked the three prettiest girls at the dance, pulled us up onto the horses and rode away with us. They had their way with us and the next day the Sheriff and a posse found us back in the mountains. They had brought a preacher with them and we were each married to the partner of the night before. My partner was Gran Riley. We have been married ever since."

That was not the only tale of violence in the family. Gran Riley, Frank's father, had a scar almost like a dimple on his cheek, Frank said that it was where his mama shot his father when she caught him cheating on her. I was fascinated by this entirely different way of life. It was way more interesting than many of the books I read, but I was ready to leave when our time was up. I did not love being a part of it.

We returned to Georgia and moved into a small house trailer that we rented. The kitchen table folded up so you could sit on the couch and watch TV and the bed had to be pulled away from the wall to make it up and then pushed back to get by it to go to the bathroom, a tiny little room that you could put your feet in the shower while you sat on the toilet. I felt like I was living in a doll house and I loved it.

There was a drive-in restaurant across the street and the big hit that they played constantly was "Wake Up Little Susie" by the Everly Brothers. I still love that song. It was the theme of a time of change and me becoming me.

Chapter 20: Virginia and Massachusetts

My beautiful son, Frank DeWayne Riley II, was born on February 20th, 1958. He was the most beautiful baby ever born in the whole wide world. There were some complications with his birth, however. I continued bleeding the whole night after he was born and went into a coma for nine days I received eight pints of blood and my sweet boy had imprinted on the nurse who fed and cared for him for that nine days. The first time I held him after I woke from the coma, he cried until the nurse came in and shushed him. He quickly adapted to me and to this day when he walks in a room, I still feel that beautiful warm feeling of love for him.

Life moved really fast after that. The squadron that Frank was in dissolved and he was sent to Langley AFB, Virginia. He drove my beloved 1942 Ford to Virginia and abandoned it on the side of the road when the radiator ran out of water and the car overheated. After finding us a place to live, he came to get me and our lovely son and we rode a train to Virginia. Suddenly I felt like a world traveler; Virginia, Ohio, Kentucky, wow! Things started to go awry with our relationship though. Frank had a temper and I was not a shy retiring person. When I defied him, he would lose his temper and slap me. The first time this happened the slap knocked my head into the corner of the door that was open and I went down like a sack of potatoes. I was horrified. I had never seen a man hit a woman before. He was always apologetic afterwards, but added that I should not talk back to him because it made him lose his temper and do things that he wasn't proud of. I found him blaming me even more appalling than the actual slap. But I was sixteen and found myself pregnant again. So, I determined to find a way to work this out.

We were only in Virginia for six weeks before Frank was shipped to Bermuda. His rank was not high enough for the Air Force to pay for me to join him, so I returned to Mother and Daddy. I did not like being back in a place where I was not in charge. It had only taken me a few months to love the independence of living in my own home. I checked the airfare to Bermuda and for my Christmas present to myself, I bought a ticket to Bermuda. Frank rented us a cottage overlooking a bay. I boarded a plane at five months pregnant, with a rambunctious ten month old boy who had just been walking one month and ran everywhere. It was a challenging flight to say the least, but I was so excited. It was an adventure. Now I was a world traveler.

In Bermuda I learned to be an adult. There were no friends and Frank never brought anyone home, nor was he friendly with the neighbors. The ladies next door on each side were kind, but I was so young and we had no common ground to build a friendship on. Frank's temper grew worse. I realize now that he must have felt totally trapped by our marriage and tried to make the best of it. I think all in all he liked me but did not like being tied down. He often erupted in angry slaps to me and Frankie, or Bobo, as he called our son. Our daughter, Colleene, was born on April 14th, 1959, in Bermuda, and we moved from our beautiful Overlook Cottage to a basement apartment in the little town of St. George's. All of the women in the apartment building were military wives and I fit right in. We played cards, gossiped, and babysat for each other. I hated the dark apartment, but I loved having people in my life again. The swapping of babysitting allowed me more freedom to shop and see the sights. The apartment building was on a tiny island. There was a dock in our front yard. Huge Canadian naval ships docked in our front yard. I was surprised to see a ship there one morning. The water was so clear there that I had thought it was only a few feet deep and there was a ship that was at least twenty feet down into the water. The sailors flirted with us and I felt pretty for the first time since I had my children.

Frank worked the night shift and slept all day. I kept the children outside most of the time. It was a lovely place to be outside. The weather was almost always beautiful. Frank claimed to have more hours to work and one of the neighbors told me they had seen him at the movies with another woman. I never even asked him about it. I just started saving money to buy my ticket home. I returned to Georgia two months before his tour of duty in Bermuda was done. My plan was to find a job and let Frank go to his next station alone.

Me and my two children must have created chaos for my mother. My brothers Robbie and Keith were eleven and nine years old at the time. Having me and my two children who were both under age two in a three -bedroom house was not ideal. My old bedroom had been turned into a den with a TV and chairs and me and my children slept on the couch in the living room. At the time, I was eighteen and naïve and believed she must be glad to have me back. We argued about everything, and I was stubborn and hardheaded as I always have been. When Frank came home from Bermuda, he told us he was reassigned to Chicopee Falls, Massachusetts. He would go ahead and find us a place to live and I could stay with mother until then. I did not argue.

I had not found a job. I did not want to go to Massachusetts. I had no idea what to do. Weeks went by and finally Frank called and said he had not found us a place yet, but mother took the phone and told him in no uncertain terms that I could not stay there any more and he needed to come get me immediately. I couldn't help but cry. My father objected and said that I could stay there as long as I wanted. Mother yelled at him. He told her that was my home and if she didn't want to take care of me, she should leave. I quickly stepped in and said I was fine. I would go as soon as Frank came to get me. He arrived that weekend and we left posthaste I now knew, if I wanted to leave him, I had to do it on my own.

My first snowfall came. I was so excited I could not sleep. It snowed eight inches. I loved shoveling the sidewalks and bundling the kids up to play in the snow. The weather stayed cold. The snow did not melt. It stayed and stayed and stayed. It got dirty and you couldn't start the car. The roads were slippery and it was too cold for the kids to play outside. I quickly became less fond of snow.

I read books, lots of books. I began reading to the children books I borrowed from a neighbor. We had only one car and I had no way to get to the library. She had no children's books. My children learned to love Tarzan and the Red Planet. My neighbor loved Edgar Rice Burroughs and we read all of his books. My son and I still cherish those stories.

I once called the police when Frank struck me. They told me there was nothing they could do since he was my husband. Frank told me he would kill me if I ever called the police again.

I found a job working on a production line at a publishing house. The work was boring, but I was with people and I was good at it. I was bored. I decided to go to a job placement service. I knew that I could not qualify for a better job if I told them I had not finished high school, so I lied. When they asked me what my GPA was, I did not know what a GPA was and told them that my overall average was about a 96% which was true, just not the part about which grade I completed. I got hired by Milton Bradley Company in the accounting department to work in the receiving office. I loved it. I received all the bills of lading and matched the quantities received and prices to the contracts, and worked out any discrepancies and then took them to the billing department. I had a job. I was making money. I could find a way to stash some money away and get free of my rapidly worsening marriage.

The funny thing is, I am not capable of being unhappy for long periods of time. I had a deep sense that I was on the right track and everything was going to work out just fine, I just needed to be patient.

Chapter 21: Food

My love affair with food began very early. I remember sitting in a high chair and my Aunt Lillian laughing because I asked for another egg. Later, when I was a toddler, we were having dinner at her house and I saw a bowl of black-eyed peas on the table and told her that was not enough black-eyed peas. She laughed and put a whole bowl of those wonderful peas by my plate. I was a discriminating eater even at that age. She made the best black-eyed peas in the world.

My desire to cook began early also. When I was about ten years old, my friend Pat Dickson and I decided to bake a cake. We found the ingredients in her mother's kitchen and a recipe book. We didn't exactly follow the recipe, however. I knew that my mother put her biscuits under the broiler to brown them on top. So, when we got impatient with the time for cooking in the cookbook was way too long, I suggested we hurry it up by turning the broiler on. It browned nicely. Then when making the icing, Pat and I tasted the vanilla flavoring and decided it was way too delicious to only put in a teaspoon full, so we dolloped in a large dose of vanilla. When we served our lopsided concoction, our parents laughed and called it our vanilla rock cake. I learned to follow directions more closely in the future.

My next adventure came about because my daddy often commented that he missed the smell of yeast bread baking. His grandmother had made yeast bread. My family made biscuits and cornbread, but neither of which used yeast. At about thirteen, I found a recipe for loaves of yeast bread. I talked mother into buying some yeast and I began. Our house was heated by a gas furnace under the house with two grates in the floor for the heat to come out of. I mixed up the ingredients as directed, but again grew impatient with the rising time. I figured that if I put the bowl on the furnace grate, the dough would rise faster. It did. The side effect was that the dough at the bottom of the bowl cooked hard without rising. We had to throw that batch out. A few days later, I succeeded in making a loaf of yeast bread. Daddy was kind and ate it without complaining, but he did advise me that I must not have followed the kneading instructions because it was pretty lumpy. I was not discouraged and kept working at it until, as an adult, my yeast rolls are the most often requested dishes for covered suppers anywhere I go.

After I met Frank, Chef Boyardee came out with a box of ingredients that was for a pizza pie. I had never heard of a pizza pie, but Frank said he loved pizzas. So I bought the mix and I loved that pizza pie. We had them often. Several years later, when we lived in Massachusetts, we lived in an Italian neighborhood and I had a real Italian pizza. I never made another Chef Boyardee pizza again. Who knew that there were more kinds of cheese than hoop cheese or cheddar cheese? Whoever even heard of pepperoni?

My next food adventures happened on my flight to Bermuda. We had to change planes in New York. I was in awe of the airport and the food stands and the number of people and was hungry. I didn't have much cash, but the food stand sign said I could get bacon and eggs well within my price range. I went to the counter and ordered my bacon and eggs. I couldn't believe my eyes when the eggs came out raw. Well not quite raw, the whites were white. I told the man the eggs were not done. He said those are sunny side up. They are raw I argued. I had never seen an egg with the yellow raw. I asked could he cook my eggs some more. He said if I paid him for another plate. I couldn't afford another plate, so I ate the bacon and toast and the whites of the eggs and gagged at the sight of the yolks running all over the plate. Some of that gagging may have been because I was five months pregnant.

On the plane from New York to Bermuda we were served lunch. Now, in 1957, airlines hired chefs to plan their meals and they were elegant. The funny thing is though that the only thing I remember about the meal is that the salad had black olives on it. I had heard of black olives but had never seen one. When I tasted that salad with those black olives, I felt that I was a wealthy world traveler and determined that in the future I would serve black olives so people would know I was grown up and ate gourmet food.

When we returned from Bermuda, our next Air Force station was in Massachusetts. What a food adventure that was! All of the salads at the restaurants had black olives and lots of different kinds of cheeses. At the corner of our street there was a deli that had rows and rows of different kinds of cheeses and different kinds of breads and different kinds of meats in big rolls that they sliced for you when you ordered them. My neighbors were Italian and they taught me how to choose which kinds of cheeses to use for which dishes. I learned to make lasagna with five different kinds of cheeses. On Fridays, the fishermen set up booths on the corner outside of where I worked where they sold two live lobsters for five dollars. I had tasted lobster once in Bermuda at a fancy restaurant where Frank took me for my eighteenth birthday. I could not believe that the only thing I had to do to make a lobster taste marvelous was drop it live into boiling water and serve it with melted butter. I splurged a lot on those lobsters and never grew tired of them. Frank complained and I had to ease up on how often I served them. But once he was out of the picture, I ate two at a time. The kids did not want to eat anything they saw me kill and I just smiled and did not try to convince them otherwise.

Once, after I moved back to Georgia with the kids, I got Sudie Fields, my mother's friend, to help me paint my bathroom. Her only request was that I feed her lunch. I got paid once a month and it was the end of the month. I really wanted to fix something special for her. I had bought a bottle of artichoke hearts at some previous time, but had not figured out how to prepare them. I didn't have enough flour in the house to make biscuits, but I did have some sliced ham and cheese. I wrapped the cheese up in the ham and battered the artichokes with the flour that I had, and fried them. Mother said Sudie told everyone she met about the gourmet meal she had eaten at my house.

As time went by, I experimented, took cooking classes, and got better. Cooking is a love and I enjoy sharing my creations with my friends and family. When I am stressed, I cook. When I am happy, I cook. When I am unhappy, I cook. It is my outlet for creativity that only takes a few hours and, being the egotist that I am, it always garners a lots of praise, which I "eat" up.

Chapter 22: The End of a Love Story

As I worked and Frank took a second job at a bowling alley, we drifted further and further apart. Our sex life, which had always been often, faltered. Frank became angrier and spent more money foolishly. He would come home on payday and bring things we could not afford: a beautiful expensive coat for Colleene, earrings and necklace for me, an archery set for himself, and finally a new Corvair Spyder Convertible which was beautiful, but way too expensive for our budget. All of these things cost a lot and did not leave enough for me to pay the rent and still buy groceries. He took out his frustrations on me and the kids. A neighbor called Family and Children's Services when they saw bruises on our son. I persuaded the Family and Children Services worker that it would not happen again, but I could not control his fits of anger. I showed up for work with a black eye. I had been schooled by Frank to tell them at work that I had fell and hit the corner of a coffee table. My sweet boss, Abraham Diamond, said I did not have to stay with an abusive husband. He and his wife were always very kind to me.

One night Frank was supposed to go to work at the bowling alley at midnight. I had fallen asleep and the alarm did not go off. Suddenly I woke up and it was a few minutes after midnight. I woke him and he was pissed. He left in a huff. We did not have a phone. About an hour later our landlady who lived downstairs was knocking at my door. She said I had a phone call. I went downstairs and answered the phone. It was a hospital in Holyoke, the town the bowling alley was in.

They told me my husband had been in a car accident and I needed to get there right away. The landlady, Mrs. Goesling, agreed to watch the children and her husband drove me to the hospital. When I arrived, Frank was in the emergency room and they were doing a tracheotomy on him when I walked in. I swooned, like a fool, and a nun caught me. It was a Catholic hospital. They immediately gave me a shot to relax me. I got drunker than a skunk on that shot. Frank's commanding officer came in and I was giggly and embarrassed that I was giggly. He was very kind and walked me around the hospital showing me some of the unusual details in the designs in the old hospital building. There were antique tiled fireplaces and moldings throughout the building. He helped me get in touch with Mr. and Mrs. Riley. Frank was brain dead, but they had him on a ventilator. He had a crushed skull where he had driven under a tractor trailer truck. They had no idea how long he would live. The Riley's wanted to know if I would pay for their gas to come. I said no. I called my mother and she flew up the next day. Someone from the base met her plane and took her to see me and then took her to the house to take on the child care responsibilities. I stayed at the hospital. When the Riley's arrived at our house, they called the hospital to get me to come home and cook something for them. I refused.

When Mrs. Riley arrived at the hospital and she told me to pray for Frank to live. I remembered the lesson I had at Vacation Bible School that we should always pray for God's will to be done. That teacher said her mother was dying and they prayed for her to live and she lived several weeks in agony. I knew Frank would not want to live as a vegetable, so I prayed for God's will to be done and Mrs. Riley was furious.

He lived for three days. On Monday, I called my boss, Abraham Diamond, and told him my husband had died in a car accident. He said "Good." I should have been offended, but I felt grateful. My first reaction to realizing that the hand I was holding was getting cold was a sense of relief that me and my children were safe. I felt guilty for feeling that. Abe gave me some validation that I was not a bad person. After a lot of therapy, a therapist finally asked me "did you want him to die or would you have been happier if he was just out of your life and you didn't have to deal with him anymore?" I realized that I just needed him to be out of my life.

Before Frank's family left, they began piling things up to take with them, like Frank's bowling ball and shoes. Then they said they would get a trailer to take the refrigerator with them. I agreed that they could have everything else they had amassed, but I would not let them have my refrigerator. They left in a huff.

We buried him in Cincinnati on October 12th, 1962. I went home with Momma and Daddy for a week and then went back to Springfield. I was treated so kindly by my boss and co-workers and I could not envision what to do next in my life. After a year I moved back to Georgia. I received a veteran's pension and social security aid for dependent children and wives. It was enough to live on if I was thrifty.

One strange story that came out of all this is that I "fixed his brakes." A few days after I returned to Massachusetts, I learned that because he drove under a tractor trailer truck, the police had investigated the brakes and me. They learned that my father had an auto body shop and had interviewed some of my neighbors and learned that Frank was sometimes abusive. They also had the report where I had called that time when he hit me. But, after all that investigation, they had determined that I was not to blame. I never saw or talked to the police and only learned about it secondhand. However, when someone told me about it, I laughed and said, "So you better not mess with me, I do know how to fix brakes." I liked the idea that nobody could ever push me around again. I found it funny that anyone could believe that I could fix brakes, much less kill somebody. But, strangely, I liked the idea that I could scare someone enough that they would think twice before hurting me or my children ever again. Almost everyone who knows me knows the mantra, "Don't mess with her, she knows how to fix brakes."

Once when my great-grandson was about eight, his mother was married to a man who had a drinking and drug problem and was becoming abusive. My grandson pulled me aside and asked me "Could you fix his brakes?" I assured him that I could not and never had really "fixed anybody's brakes," but I would try to help him get away from that situation, and I did. But just be warned, I might really know how to fix brakes, so don't mess with me or mine.

Chapter 23: Preconceived Notions

When I went to Massachusetts, I encountered a lot of people who loved to hear me talk in my southern accent. I loved to hear the different accents in them, too. There was the Boston "paaak the car" and the beautiful lyrical accents of Italy in my Italian neighborhood. They loved to hear me say "oyul" for oil, as they pronounced it "all."

In my job at Milton Bradley, I matched the delivery slips with the orders for the product and the invoices received with the prices on the orders, then delivered the invoices to the accounting department for payment. Since I had lied about my education to get the job, I was very conscientious about completing each task. One thing that helped me with my confidence was efficiency studies that we were required to complete each week. We were given a form that allotted a certain amount of time for each task that we completed. As time went on, I had gradually increased my efficiency so that each week I was now completing my forty hours of work on Wednesday afternoon or Thursday morning. One day when delivering the invoices to the accounting department, one of the items on a particular invoice was for ½ pints of milk that were on the break cart each day. The dairy sent out a notice that they were increasing the price of the ½ pints of milk by ½ cent. Naturally, that made a very small difference in the total price of the invoice. I checked the amount of milk delivered, multiplied by the new price and delivered the invoice for payment. An accounting clerk called me to her desk and loudly proclaimed that I had not caught an error in the billing for the milk and had sent an incorrect invoice for payment. I asked her had she looked at the attachment. She said, "so what?" I pointed to the attached statement to the invoice that said they had raised the price by ½ cent. She quickly sat down and recalculated the price and looked up at me in surprise. "You don't think nearly as slowly as you talk, do you?" she asked. I was truly stunned that anyone would think I was mentally slow. I had not ever been accused of being mentally slow before. This poor woman had assumed because of my accent that I was mentally delayed or close thereto. I have laughed at this story many times and I think of it when I am tempted to determine what a person is like before I know them. You cannot judge by color, accent, clothing, size, sex, or any of those other variables what a person is like until you know more about them. That was not the last time I was judged wrongly by my place of birth, gender, or other nonsensical thing, but it was the funniest.

Chapter 24: Nicknames

Different families have different traditions about nicknames. My dad's family was fond of nicknames. His Aunt Mae always called daddy "Mary" and his sister Helen "Boatin'." They always shyly smiled at her when she used these nicknames. I know they had a special meaning for them, but when I asked, they always brushed me off.

My father called me Pennywinkle. When I found out it was a very wiggly worm that was especially good for fishing, I asked him why he called me the name of a wiggly worm. He said when I was little and sometimes slept with him and Mama I wiggled the whole night.

Frank called our son "Bobo" and our daughter "Po'k Chop." I don't know the origin of Bobo, but Po'k Chop came from her cute little fat cheeks when she was little. It seems that nicknames or other variations of names are required when the son is a namesake of the father. My grandson was named Philip Dale Smith Jr. When he was young, he was called Little Dale.

At some point many children rebel against their nicknames. I rebelled when I learned a Pennywinkle was a worm, but after talking to daddy about the origin it always made me feel the tenderness of sleeping in a warm bed with my parents when I was tiny. So I relented and cherished that nickname as it was an expression of closeness when it was used by my mother or father and I felt myself using the same shy smiles that I remembered from my childhood when Aunt Mae used those nicknames for daddy and Helen.

However, Philip Dale and Frank II rebelled much more strongly. When my son Bobo (Frank II) was five years old, he informed me in a very determined little voice that his name was Frank and he no longer wanted to be called Bobo. If I called him Bobo, he studiously ignored me. He quickly trained me to call him Frank. My mother was not so easily trained, and called him Bobo off and on forever. I think she enjoyed making him uncomfortable and eventually Frank came to have that same shy smile that I knew so well when she addressed him as Bobo.

Colleene's fat cheeks melted and the name Po'k Chop evaporated. Philip Dale demanded he be called Philip, and since he was no longer little, Little Dale disappeared.

When I was dating Ed many years later someone referred to him as an "asshole." He quickly jumped in and told them they could not call him that. He said, "That is Peggy's pet name for me." It got a big laugh, but it was not exactly true.

When I think of my son as a little boy, I often picture that determined little stance of his when I called him Bobo and he was refusing to answer me. I liked the way he handled that transition. He didn't fuss or rant or cry, he told me not to call him that and then refused to answer to it until he had retrained me. I have tried to emulate that procedure many times in my life. Just make a plan, make sure the important people know what the plan is so there will be no misunderstanding, then stick to the plan until your goal is accomplished. It doesn't always work but there is not much of a fuss in the process.

Part III: Finding Me

Chapter 25: Home Again

The Air Force agreed to pay my moving costs to anywhere I wanted to move in the United States as long as it was within one year of the date my husband had died. I loved Massachusetts and intended to stay there, but things gradually changed. My sweet Bobo (Frank II) began to stop men on the street and ask them, "Will you be my daddy?" I was attending a church that offered counseling. I went to see the minister and he asked if I had family with males that my son could bond with. I assured him that I had a father and two brothers. He advised me that it would probably be best for my son if he lived near them.

I began making plans to return to Warner Robins. Abe said the president of Milton Bradley wanted to speak with me. I had only met him once before and was not sure what to expect. The time before was after I had gouged his son in the belly with my elbow. After I became a widow, some of the men at work had begun to view me differently. The president's son had begun to walk up behind me and put his arm around me. I told him to stop. One day he came up behind me, put his arm around me and I gave him a good jab in the stomach with my elbow. He was furious. So, when his father called me into his office, I had gone with some trepidation. Imagine my surprise when he laughed and said, "Good for you. Some woman needs to put him in his place."

He stood when I entered the room this time and asked me to be seated. "We were worried about you when your husband died. I had asked the nurse to keep an eye on you to make sure you were okay. She reports to me that you had a rough few weeks when you came back, but that you are really doing well now. We are all really proud of you. I would ask you to stay and offer an incentive, but I understand your need to be nearer your family. If you ever need a reference for a new job, please do not hesitate to use me as a reference."

I was overwhelmed. Then he took a book off of the shelf behind him. "This is a book I wrote about the history of Milton Bradley, Inc. I have signed it and would like for you to have it as a reminder of your time here, which I hope you remember fondly." I thanked him profusely almost in tears and walked back to Abe's office where everyone hugged me and gave me good wishes for my future. I was off to Georgia and a new chapter in my life.

I rented a little two bedroom house on the other side of town from my family. Bobo and Po'k Chop were happy in their new home. Daddy, Robbie, and Keith spent a lot of time with them and they thrived. Mother and Colleene bonded. Now it was time to sit down to decide what to do next. Since I had no luck before moving to Massachusetts finding a job in Warner Robins, and there was no toy factory nearby, I needed a new set of skills. I decided to finish high school. I knew I could take the GED and get a certificate that was semi-equivalent to a high school diploma, but I felt I had missed out on being a teenager and I wanted the classroom experience of learning and to go to a prom and a football game and hang out with groups of teenagers. At that time people who had been married and/or had children were not allowed to attend public schools in Houston County, Georgia, without special permission. So, I had a session with the school board and was advised that there would be absolutely no talking about sex, childbirth, or anything of that nature. We could not contaminate these young minds, I agreed. And one week after school had started for the year, I was allowed to enter eleventh grade at the newly opened Northside High School in Warner Robins, Georgia. My children were in day care at Mrs. Adams Nursery and I could be a semi-teenager at age twenty-one. I was elated.

It was time for a new life and a new adventure.

Chapter 26: High School at 21

I loved school, from first grade in the closet to tenth grade where I made straight 100's for six weeks in algebra class. Northside High School was no different, except that I was now twenty-one years old and had two children. There were a few glitches. One of the girls in my class was the daughter of one of mother's friends. I had known her since we were both little. She was six years younger than me, but she took me under her wing and one night we went to a drive-in hamburger joint to flirt with the boys. She flirted, I watched. The boys were six years younger than me and I was "not going there." Several of the boys hopped in the back seat of my car and we laughed and talked. Then another boy joined the group and started talking about having sex with me. I asked him to get out of my car. He said, "You can't make me." I threatened to lock the doors and drive over a cliff, with me jumping out before it went over. He slammed out of the car, leaned over me in the window and said something about wishing he could give me some babies. I don't remember what happened next.

The next thing I remember is being at home and crying to my brother, Robbie, about this awful boy. Robbie said, "I will put a stop to this" and jumped into his car and left. He returned in about an hour. He asked me what I had done to that boy. I said I drove off. "Well," he said, "you must have blacked out."

"What?" I said.

"Everyone there was talking about the girl who threw Bucky all over the parking lot with some judo throws. The girl they described was you." Frank had attempted to teach me some judo throws, but when I dropped him mid-throw and he twisted his ankle, he had

89

stopped teaching me. I guess I remembered the lessons better than I thought. I still do not remember even getting out of the car, much less throwing poor Bucky all over the lot.

There were a group of boys at school that stood at the bottom of the stairwell and tried to look up the girls' skirts as they ascended the stairs. On Monday, when I started up the stairs, one of them made some rude remark, one of the other boys quickly shushed him. "That's the girl that threw Bucky across the parking lot Friday night. You better not make her mad." None of the boys ever spoke rudely to me again. My one regret is that I don't remember that moment of triumph over the heckling.

School was wonderful. I was almost the same age as some of my teachers, but I treated them respectfully and they were kind to me. My history teacher was an old war veteran whose head was scarred from burns he received in WWII. He was a great teacher, but he never called on me in class. After several months, he asked me to stay after class. I was nervous. He didn't put up with any shenanigans in class and I didn't have any idea what I had done wrong. I sat in my seat as he resettled behind his desk. "I told them I would not have you in my class when they assigned you to me," he said. I was not shocked by this statement, but wondered where he was going with this. "I was wrong," he said. "You are a good student and an asset to the class and I apologize if I have made you uncomfortable." I almost cried. I think a lot of the school staff and teachers had some trepidations about me but I think they all came to feel the same way he did. I was always treated fairly and kindly. When I go to class reunions now, everybody knows me and tells me about how my need to go back to school made them realize how important an education was, or they just laugh and tell stories about me to each other. It was an important decision in my life and I have never regretted it.

I graduated seventh in my class, went to the junior and senior proms with dates that were in the Air Force, and was asked to give a speech at our graduation. The graduation ceremony was outside. As I gathered my notes to give my speech, a moth flew into my face. I swatted at the moth and my notes went flying into the audience. I forgot my speech and was tongue-tied for a moment. Then I just thanked the students and teachers for all the kindnesses they had shown me. I got all teary eyed while doing it and I saw a few tears in the audience. Some of the students only remember me giving a speech at graduation and think that I was the valedictorian. I cannot bring myself to disillusion them.

I made friends from that class that have remained my friends to this day. It was a wonderful transition from being married to learning to live on my own. It paved the way for jobs that I didn't have to lie to get, and college and a realization that friends can be any age.

Chapter 27: My Son Frank's Stories

On Mother's Day in 2021, I had a lovely visit from my son Frank, formerly known as Bobo. We spent several hours talking about his memories of some of the stories I have told and other memories of our life together. Some I had heard and some I had only known partially. One that was totally new to me was of a visit to my Aunt Helen's when he was about fifteen. By my best calculations, Helen's daughter Cathy was about twenty or twenty-one at the time. He said he gladly joined me on the visit to Aunt Helen's because he had a crush on his cousin Cathy. She was the cutest funniest young woman he had ever met. He was so disappointed when we arrived and she was not there. After I had gone to bed she came in and he had a little time with her and has cherished the memory of that time spent with her.

One train of thought was of all the scares we had endured together. When we first moved back to Warner Robins, one of our favorite things to do that summer was go swimming at a Lake near Macon called Vinson Valley. They had a sliding board that the bigger kids were having so much fun on that he begged me to let him go down it. With great trepidation I allowed my five year old son to climb that great tall ladder and come down that board. I waited at the bottom of the slide to catch him because the water at the bottom was almost over his head. The child before Frank went down head first. Frank in his too grownup mind saw that going down head first made the boy go down much faster and Frank, in all the wisdom of a five year old, immediately chose to go down head first. I was caught off guard and could not back up fast enough to catch him on his new trajectory. His little head hit me in the mouth so hard, it knocked me under the water.

My teeth had put a gash in his forehead that was bleeding profusely. People gathered immediately to rescue this poor bleeding boy. He says he was frantically looking for me because I was still submerged. When I came up, total panic seized me. He was covered in blood and yelling for his mama at the top of his voice. I pushed my way in, soothed him as best I could with my own panic rising. Someone handed me a cloth and we made our way to the car. He had stitches in his head at the base hospital and all was well.

A few years later, he was probably ten by then, he came home from the pool in our neighborhood and called for his stepfather, John, to come in the bathroom with him. He pulled down his pants and showed John a hole in his leg where he had jumped across a ditch and been impaled by a broken limb. I walked in the bathroom, took one look at the leg, and left to call the doctor. John yelled at me, "Don't leave me in here with this hole." I calmly loaded my son in the car and drove him to the base hospital where they immediately took him into the surgery room with me trailing behind. The doctor looked at the hole, put on some gloves, and ran one finger into the hole, shook his head and then ran two fingers into the hole. I woke up on the floor with a nurse trying to get me up. The doctor cleaned out the wound, inserted a lot of gauze, and sewed up the hole leaving a little gauze sticking out. We had to pull a little gauze out each day to allow the hole to gradually close up. I don't remember Frank ever complaining or crying. He said he didn't want to worry me. From the time his father died, he always felt it was his job to take care of me.

One of the stories we laughed about occurred a few years after his leg healed. John was on an all-night Ham Radio Jamboree and Frank, Colleene, and I were in bed asleep. I heard the front door open. I called, "Is that you John?" No answer. "Is that you, Robbie?" My brother was a welcomed guest and often walked in unannounced, sometimes late at night. I yelled "Frank, are you awake?"

"Yes, ma'am," he answered.

The footsteps were coming down the hall towards our bedrooms. "Well, get your gun and shoot whoever that is coming down the hall."

"Yes ma'am," he answered in a really calm voice like he had received a military command. We heard the footsteps running back down the hall and the front door slam as whoever was there departed hastily. Frank came out of his room carrying his BB gun and we sat on the floor and giggled with relief.

He was so quick to understand and so willing to be there for me that I always felt safe when he was around and still do. It is such a joy to have a lifetime friend that is your own child. It makes you feel like God was looking out for you when he gave you this special child.

Chapter 28: Abraham Diamond

As I previously said, Abe, my wonderful boss at Milton Bradley, was my stalwart friend when I was going through the process of dealing with Frank's death. He and his wife were determined that I should put that marriage behind me and move forward. Frank died on October 2nd. For Thanksgiving, I received a box with a turkey and all the fixings from the Salvation Army. Me and my little son and daughter ate until we were about to burst on Thanksgiving day and enjoyed being all by ourselves with our new bounty. Shortly after that, Abe started talking about the Christmas Party at Milton Bradley insisting that I attend. I thought it was too soon to attend a fancy dress ball after my husband's death. Abe got his wife to call me and take me shopping for a beautiful party dress. That dress was a shimmering aquamarine marvel that made me look like a million dollars. I could not resist dreaming of going to a ball in that beautiful confection. Then he introduced me to a single girl that worked at Milton Bradley. He said that I didn't have to go with a date because this beautiful, sweet girl and I could go together and every single guy in the place would dance with us. I didn't know how to dance. With all of my newfound independence I found a dance studio that taught dancing lessons and signed up. With my newfound confidence and my beautiful new friend, I went to dances at the base. I planned and a new world opened up for me. I felt pretty.

Abraham Diamond was a marvel. He had started the first toy worker's union. The management at Milton Bradley had then promoted him to a management position so that he could no longer be a union member, but he continued to work closely with the union to protect the workers. At Christmas each year, Milton Bradly Co. held a Christmas party for all the workers and their families in which each child was given a toy made by Milton Bradley and a bag of goodies. Of course, Santa gave out these gifts. Even though Abe was a Jew, he loved the role of Santa and that Saturday afternoon party was one of the highlights each year. That evening was the Christmas Ball, a full-dress ball, with music and food. I had never been to anything as generous and delightful as the party for the kids nor anything as elegant as the ball. I felt like Cinderella. It was a fairy tale come true. I danced (that sinful thing my mother had ingrained in me to avoid). I did not feel any unholy feelings when the men from the office danced with me and their wives smiled on. I only felt pretty and happy.

I was adjusting to living alone with my children. I had never lived alone before. Even though I thought I was prepared to leave Frank, the day-to-day living was emptier than I had expected. As Christmas neared, I dreaded being alone on Christmas Eve and Christmas Day. Many people had invited me to share the day with them, but I really wanted to figure out how to be me with just my kids and Christmas seemed like the first challenge. I woke up Christmas morning excited about the little presents I had bought for the kids and I had planned a full Christmas dinner. But, I felt totally alone and began to cry before the kids woke up. Then the doorbell rang. I hurriedly put on my housecoat and answered the door. At the door stood three of the engineers from Milton Bradley who developed new toys to market. They grinned, and started carrying in toys. "Abe told us that we should bring you all of the toys we developed this year that the company decided were not marketable." By this time, the kids were awake. These wonderful engineers demonstrated to my little ones how to use each one of the toys they had brought. Then they gave us all a hug and waved goodbye. Recently when my sweet son Frank and I were talking about his childhood, he remembered one of those toys and how special he felt when he had a toy none of the other kids had ever seen.

Because our car was totally destroyed in the accident that Frank was in, I was left with no transportation. Abe called a friend of his who had a car dealership and his friend sold me a lavender used Dodge in perfect running order for two hundred and fifty dollars. I loved that car. It had gold flecked seat covers and push button drive. It was reliable and ran smoother than my old Ford.

There were many, many other people who helped me and my children as we adjusted to a new life. I will always think of them and Springfield, Massachusetts, as a people and a place who nurtured this little Georgia cracker when I was learning how to fly on my own. Life has downturns for all of us, but the people like Abe and his lovely wife, who helped me through those low spots, prove over and over again how kind humans can be to each other.

Chapter 29: Dating Again

1963 was an eventful year. I restarted high school in the eleventh grade at the age of twenty-one, moved back to my old home town of Warner Robins, Georgia, and began dating again. When I met Frank, I was fifteen years old, and had dated a grand total of two other dates. One was a hayride and one was with a boy who had a car and was totally shocked that I had never kissed a boy before. He quickly disappeared from my life with no regrets from me. Now, I had two children, ages three and four, and was a widow with very little experience with the dating game.

Dating was made possible by my wonderful brother, Robbie, who at sixteen, had taken on the task of loving me with all his heart. This included free babysitting any time I asked. When not dating, I cooked for him, we laughed and played cards, went places with the kids, and thoroughly enjoyed each other's company.

With this newfound freedom, I explored the USO. It was an atmosphere of clean fun where I got to use my new found skills at dancing. I was a hit. It surprised me. I never wanted for dance partners or dates. From this broad selection of eligible bachelors who were all in the Air Force, I selected a young man from New Orleans named Robert Mehan. He was cute and smart and immediately became friends with Robbie and my mother. He was a fantastic Scrabble player and impressed my mother and my aunt Carolyn who both loved playing Scrabble. He was my date to my junior prom. The girls I went to school with oohed and aahed over this handsome airman at the ball, but, I was in no hurry to settle down and he became one of many airman that I dated and "broke their heart." I like to believe I broke a few hearts, much better than the other way around.

About the middle of my senior year in high school, I met John Burdge. He was a quieter sort and not as handsome as some of the others. After five years with a husband that was so handsome women turned and followed him down the street sometimes, I felt safer with this quiet man. I graduated in June of 1965 and married John on June 12th, 1965, in the Mormon church.

After being shunned by the church I had attended when meeting Frank, I had searched for a church that was warm and welcoming. While in Massachusetts, I had studied with the Jehovah Witnesses and felt loved while there, but when I moved to Warner Robins, I decided to venture out. I found the Mormon church and loved the way they emphasized family. One of the basic tenets of their faith was that each family had a family night where they played games and listened to each other. I wasn't sure I believed Joseph Smith was a prophet or that my dead relatives needed to be baptized by a descendant of someone baptized by Joseph Smith. I talked it over with the Bishop and he said that all people had questions and God would work it out. So, I was baptized by a descendant of someone baptized by Joseph Smith and began teaching a Sunday School class about religions of the world. I loved the thought that a church would encourage its parishioners to study other religions.

A new Bishop was assigned to our district and in conversations with him, he determined that it was not tolerable for anyone to be teaching a Sunday School class that did not believe that Joseph Smith was a true prophet. I saw what he meant and shortly after marrying John, I left the Mormon church. After all I could only be sealed to one husband in heaven and the men could be sealed to multiple wives. My children still attended the church and when they came home and told me that I had to get back into the church or they would not be allowed to go to heaven, or some similar nonsense, I wrote the Bishop about how I felt the church should allow me to be sealed to two husbands since neither of them had ever had another wife. I got a registered letter from the Bishopric informing me that I had been excommunicated. HA! That was the end of my Mormon adventure. My children were also encouraged to find other churches to attend and they often went to different churches with their friends.

Part IV: A New Beginning

Chapter 30: Wedding #2

The date was set: June 12th, 1965. Graduation was over. I was now a high school graduate, twenty-three years old, and ready for the next adventure. John's mother, two sisters, and a brother had arrived from New Jersey. What a delightful surprise! His mother was a beautiful redhead. His sisters were teenagers and full of excitement about the wedding. His brother was just a few years older than my children and he was delightful. They had arrived the day before the wedding. We had all found a place to sleep in my tiny two bedroom rented house, except for John who slept in his quarters on base.

Sudie Fields, my mother's friend, had finished painting my bathroom a few days before and all the paint seemed to be dry. John's mother was a trained opera singer, so she had agreed to sing for me in the wedding. John planned to dress at my house, and so his mother, siblings, my children and I piled into their car and left before he arrived so that he would not see me in my wedding dress before the ceremony. We arrived at the church and met my parents and brothers there. After introductions everyone got along beautifully. I think my brother, Robbie, immediately fell in "love" with John's older sister, Francie. Daddy was uncomfortable in a suit and had not put on a tie. He assured me that he would put it on soon. Mother fussed and fiddled with my dress. We waited. We waited. We waited. After fifteen minutes past the time set for the ceremony, John had still not arrived. I went into the room to wait for my time to be called to walk down the aisle with quite a bit of trepidation. Finally at twenty-seven minutes past the original time, Mrs. Burdge (Anne Marie) came in, hugged me, and said the ceremony was about to start. A few minutes later daddy arrived at the door with his tie on and walked me down the aisle. Anne Marie began singing. John had told me she had a trained operatic voice. I didn't know exactly what that meant until I heard her sing. It was amazing. I teared up at the beauty of her singing. What a wonderful surprise! Daddy gave me away, walked back to his place on the front row, and immediately took off his tie. I smiled at him. Hating a tie like he did, he had worn it long enough to get the job done and then felt free to be himself again. I loved him so much, tears came again.

We were married. We all went over to my parents' house for the reception which was a combination reception and birthday party for my brother, Robbie. My wedding cake read "Happy Birthday Robbie." What a beautiful thrifty day. I felt loved and cherished.

Mrs. Burdge, that was my new name: Mrs. Peggy Patricia Barrett Riley Burdge. I was a new person with a new life with a beautiful new family that were happy to have me join their family. I got lots of hugs and watched as my children were pampered and played with.

Later, John explained that the handle had fallen off the door in the bathroom and that he had to climb out the bathroom window. He had gotten some white paint on his black suit and had to find something to remove the paint before he left for the church. He apologized for scaring the bejeezus out of me by being so late to the wedding, but it made a wonderful story to tell later.

His family left, and Kay Simmons, one of the girls I knew from school agreed to stay at my house with the kids for a week and we were off to our honeymoon in Asbury Park, New Jersey.

His mother had rented an old country farmhouse that rambled everywhere and we had a room snuggled under the roof. We had privacy up there and when we wanted company, the chaos of the big houseful of his siblings, dogs, and cats was wonderful. The beach was about five miles away. What more could one ask for a perfect honeymoon? It was a perfect honeymoon.

Chapter 31: New Husband, New Life

Upon our return to Warner Robins, we started our new adventure. With my new skills acquired in high school, I was hired at Robins Air Force Base as a secretary. I could type sixty words a minute and take dictation thanks to a very patient kind secretarial skills teacher, Mrs. Holland, who stayed after class to help me practice my shorthand. I went to work in the safety office in an off-base building that was only four blocks from our house. I now made a thousand dollars a year more than I had at Milton Bradley. I was in high cotton.

One funny thing about my new job was the name of the man in charge of the safety office, Mr. Hazard. I have often seen jokes made about appropriate or inappropriate names of people in association with their jobs, and I always think of Mr. Hazard.

I guess it was a prestigious thing to have a secretary instead of a clerk typist, but not a requirement to be able to give dictation. In the whole year that I worked in that office, I was never given dictation. At first, I worried about losing my steno skills and sometimes just wrote whatever was said around me in shorthand, but after a while, I just let that skill slip away. I worried occasionally about the next job, if I got promoted, would require it, but life has a way of getting on without too much worry about that kind of thing. As it turned out, when I got a promotion to GS-4 in Recycling and Reclamations, my new boss never gave dictation either.

A short while after I got promoted, John was shipped to the Philippines. Again, his rank was not high enough to qualify for his wife to accompany him on the Air Force expense. Additionally, wives were discouraged from going to the Philippines. The Vietnam War was going on and a lot of the air support was provided from Clark AFB in the Philippines. Before John left, we had moved to a three-bedroom house and settled into a routine.

There are always wrinkles to iron out in new marriages and having two children thrown into the mixture adds extra pressure. Is the new husband allowed to discipline? What do the children call him? With John one of the big wrinkles was that he was not a morning person. He tried to make me responsible for getting him out of bed in the morning. He ignored the alarm when it went off and fussed at me when he was running late for work. I absolutely refused to be responsible for that. When he learned to get up on his own after the alarm went off and breakfast was on the table, he yelled at the kids because they were making too much noise. I resolved that issue by serving him instant oatmeal in bed. It made mornings much more pleasant for all.

When he had left for the Philippines, I missed him. There were recruiters on the base recruiting secretaries that could get Top Secret clearances to work in war offices in the Philippines. I thought, wow, I can do that. Government, being government, the recruiter quickly informed me that as a lowly airman's wife, I was not qualified for this deal. I was not to be dissuaded. I had to have a visa. The Philippine Embassy in Washington would not issue me a visa as an airman's wife. When I called and asked why they whispered that the embassy in San Francisco was quick to issue visas to enlisted men's wives if they showed up in person at the embassy with all the necessary paperwork. She faxed me a list of the paperwork required and I started planning. John tried to discourage me. He had been warned that the base frowned on wives coming on their own.

I sold my car to my mother for enough money to buy round trip tickets for me and my children, rounded up all the paperwork required, and talked to a friend of mine who lived in Oakland, California. She welcomed me and took me to the embassy and I was immediately provided with a visa for me and my children. Then my lovely friend, Gladys Green, took us sightseeing in San Francisco. We ate at Fisherman's Wharf, toured Chinatown, and returned exhausted to her house for dinner and ice cream. We fell asleep exhausted and happy.

The next day we went to the zoo. It took two days to get a flight out and we had a stopover in Hawaii. There was beauty and kindness everywhere. The flight attendants on the flight were so very kind. At one point they came and took the children with them and told me to lie down across the three seats and get some sleep.

John met us in Manila. Getting through immigration was quick and efficient. Since we arrived in the early morning, when we got to Clark AFB, it was still early afternoon. We had lunch at the Airman's/NCO club, then John suggested I check in at the employment office. The employment office was a surprise. They wanted me to go to work that day. I signed all the paperwork and agreed to start work on Monday. It was Thursday afternoon by this time. We went to our new apartment that was in the off-base housing area for officers. It seems our particular apartment did not pass inspection, so it was not considered to be a military unit.

On Monday, the children were in school, and I was sent to a Top-Secret Security underground bunker. Colonel Sterling, Major Adams, and Chief Warrant Officer McHenry were happy to have me. It seems they had been without secretarial help for several weeks and had not had much hope of a quick replacement.

Since we were in the military housing area, the base school bus picked the children up each day. The buses were painted with cartoon characters and the children were told that when school was out each day, they should look for the Mickey Mouse that was on their bus. We quickly hired a housemaid to be there when they got home. The housemaid, Angel, was paid six dollars a week. I found that appallingly cheap, but when I talked to some of my neighbors, they dared me to set a higher standard by paying more. Angel was not unhappy, so I complied.

Chapter 32: Philippine Stories

Life in the Philippines was very interesting. The weather was hot, steamy, and buggy. Flowers and flowering trees were always in bloom. We slept with nets over the bed and ceiling fans in every room. No window panes, just shutters.

Our first spat in our new paradise was when John told me to never go to downtown Angeles City without him and who have I ever allowed to order me around? The first weekend we were there he was on duty as a punishment for allowing me, a lowly airman's wife, to dare to defy everyone and come to the Philippines knowing the AIR FORCE POWERS THAT BE did not wish for me to be there. Never mind that they had immediately hired me as a secretary upon my arrival.

I took his absence as an invitation to explore and piled the children into the car and went to Angeles City. It was so exciting. The roads and streets were crowded with hustle and bustle and jeepneys everywhere. Traffic seemed to have its own rules. When I parked, little boys came running up asking me to pay them to watch my car so that nothing would be taken. They wanted five cents. I thought they were so cute, I gladly paid. I walked through rows of vegetables and fruits, some I recognized, some I didn't. Tailor shops offered to make me a dress from any picture I brought from a magazine and little bamboo shacks offered pineapple halves covered with pineapple cubes and other fruits that I didn't recognize. These confections were only a quarter. The kids and I indulged in some pineapple and were awed by all the strange sights. We returned home just as John was coming in from work. He started yelling about how he had told me not to go downtown. The kids disappeared some place safe. I stood there quietly until he ran out of steam. Then said, firmly but quietly, "you are my husband, not my father, boss, or commander." And I walked off. He never said another word about what I could or couldn't do. I guess he recognized a lost cause when he saw it.

I loved my new job. All three of the men I worked with were on flight status for bomb runs over Vietnam, so I often had weeks at a time in my quiet below ground bunker all by myself. I usually had work to do for only a couple of days after they left and then brought in novels to read. Hawaii by James Michener was a nice long novel that lasted two or three of their trips. They had set aside a bathroom just for me, since I was the only woman in the building. They gleefully put a sign on the door, instead of WOMEN it said PB4U2P: Peggy Burdge For You To Pee. I loved it. They taught me a protocol to observe when I was alone in the bunker. They showed me photos of all the people who were allowed to enter the bunker when they were not there. The dignitaries included the Base Commander, the Colonel who was the supervisor over the bunker staff, and other base dignitaries. One day, when they had been gone over a week, the buzzer sounded and I went up the stairs to observe who was at the door. There was a man with all kinds of lightening and things on his cap and he was with a whole entourage. I assumed he was a general, but he was not the general that they had shown me a photo of, so I refused to let them in. They yelled and swore, but I told them that my protocol demanded that I recognize the people I admitted to the bunker and I did not recognize any of them.

When my Lt. Col. Sterling returned, he came in grinning. "I have been dragged over the carpet this morning," he said. It seems the new base commander planned an overview of his new command and included this bunker on his route and you refused him entry.

"Yes sir," I said. "You told me not to let anyone in I didn't know."

"Didn't you read the papers all about our new commander arriving?" he asked. "No sir," I said.

"Well, I have been commanded to fire you for insubordination," he said.

"I was obeying your instructions to the letter," I said feeling a tear rising up and fighting it for all I was worth. I wanted to appear strong and righteous, not like a weak crybaby.

He softened and smiled again, "I made a compromise. You have an appointment to meet my boss and the general in fifteen minutes. I finally got them to agree that in fact you were doing precisely what you were trained to do. It was my job to make certain that you knew any changes of personnel that were authorized admittance. I just was caught up in my plans for the Vietnam raid and did not think that you might not be aware of the change of command. I will make certain in the future that the base paper will be part of your reading material in the office. Does that work for you?"

"Yes, Sir!" and I caught him off guard with a big hug. I met all the Important people that afternoon in a very quick pass through the general's staff meeting.

Life went on. There was some unrest in the Philippines, natives that resented the American presence. Occasionally there would be demonstrations at the entry gate to the base and one night as I was driving home from work, I saw one of the big riding mowers that kept the perimeter fence clear, stop and the driver get off the mower and bent over, looked down, and then began running. Soon all traffic was stopped and Air Police vehicles were racing to the scene. After the police arrived traffic began to move again. The next day at work I learned that the man on the mower had discovered a severed head that had been thrown over the fence. There were moments when I felt unsafe, but mostly life went on and I enjoyed the rhythm of the slow afternoons in the heat and the welcome relief of sundown. I had a full-time maid, a yard boy who kept the yards neat and scrubbed and waxed the floors. Life was easy and relaxed generally.

There was a mountain resort with a small base set up for rest and relaxation for the military members based in the Philippines. It was called Baguio. One weekend, John and I, along with the kids and some friends, planned a trip to this resort. It was a beautiful climb up a narrow steep winding road that our old car had some difficulty in getting us up. At places, the car ground down to 25mph at top speed. It was truly an adventure.

That night we all went to a night club where children were welcome. My son, Frank, was in third grade, nine years old, but taller than many of the native women. The sexy little singer that night was beautiful. Her voice was enchanting. She came off the stage and sang to several men at several tables, but at our table she sang to my son. He blushed and I thought he would be shy, but when she invited him to dance with her, he immediately jumped up and took her hand. She danced a few steps with him, kissed him on the cheek and returned to the stage. He was teased for many years for his first kiss being from an older woman. He always smiled a happy smile when teased this way.

Most of the cars in the Philippines were cars left there by departing military members. Our car was an old woody station wagon that had seen its better days. The headliner was tattered and hung down in some places and there was rust everywhere, but it got us around with just a few glitches here and there. One day it was making some strange rattles and we were headed to the base garage to have it checked out. As we turned the corner to go into the garage our right front tire came off and rolled into the garage ahead of us. We had enough momentum to roll in behind it before the right front end settled to the ground. Every mechanic in the garage stood for a moment in amazement and then burst out laughing. We couldn't help laughing with them. How often would you have such a mishap at such an appropriate time?

Several months before our planned departure, the yard boy, Bert, offered to take Frank to experience the planting of rice. I thought it would be a great experience for him and he was excited at the thought of seeing where Angel and Bert lived and how rice was planted in the rice paddies.

Bert assured me that they would have to take the train in order to get there early enough to plant the rice. So, with eight dollars and my son, they left at six o'clock to go on an adventure. He had warned me that they would not return until after dark so I was not worried when they showed up at eight o'clock that evening. What did confound me though, was that my son was drunk as a skunk, giggling, and wobbling. Bert made himself scarce very quickly. When Frank awoke the next day, the most that I could make of his story was that they spent most of the day in a bar with lots of pretty women and only visited Bert's and Angel's Nipa Hut for a little while, then walked to the rice paddy, said hello to everyone, then went back to the bar before being given a ride back in Bert's friend's Jeepney. There was no train trip. The money I had given them bought a lot of beer for Bert, Frank, and Bert's male and female friends. It wasn't the kind of educational experience I had envisioned for my son, but I could not deny that it was a very educational experience.

After fourteen months of a lot of very educational experiences for us all, I returned home in time for Christmas and John was shipped back to the States in February and finished his period of Air Force service. Another chapter of our life began to unfold in Warner Robins, Georgia.

Chapter 33: Marriage to John

We moved into a rental house and John and I began to discover what settled living was about. He bought a Ham Radio set and began studying for his Ham Radio license. The kids were enrolled in a school nearby, Miller Hills Elementary. I got a job on the base in the Base Employment Office and we developed a slow quiet rhythm. Something was amiss. John took every opportunity to stay in his closet radio room and I was bored so I began to take some college courses at night which the base gladly paid for.

Frank was having problems at school. The teacher asked us to come talk to her. She explained that Frank slept in class. Not just laying his head on the desk, but he would actually lay down on the floor and was not rude but would not get up when she asked him to. On her recommendation, we decided to take him to a child psychologist. The psychologist tested his IQ and told us some of the problem might be boredom since his IQ was very high. He also said there was some problem with his relationship with John and felt that if John and I insisted on him calling John dad or some nickname other than John that they might bond better. John called the doctor a quack and worked on convincing me that Frank was just really smart and we needed to spend more time involving him in challenging opportunities. To keep the peace and because it seemed to make some sort of sense, I agreed.

Frank seemed to be better. One day we went by the playground to pick him up and found him standing with a policeman. When we joined them, the policeman said he had a call that Frank was bullying a boy and they were waiting for the boy and his father to show up. Frank was angry. "He called me a son of a," he fussed.

"A son of a what?" the officer asked.

"Just a son of a," Frank whined.

Just then a man and a boy twice Frank's size walked up.

"Is this the big boy you said was bullying you?" the father asked his son.

With head hanging low, the boy answered. "Yes, sir."

"You said he was bigger than you." The father started turning red, and turned to us. "I am so sorry. I really thought he was in danger." He turned and grabbed his son and started marching away.

The officer turned to us and we all began laughing. I hugged Frank to me. I liked my son that refused to be bullied by a boy twice as big as he was and never ever told us how big the boy was, only that he had been called what he considered to be an insult. Neither of them even knew what the whole statement should have been to be a real insult. Just boys being boys.

We bought a house with a room for John's radio equipment, and separate rooms for each of the children, and went back to the routine of work, ham radio, and college at night. My brother Robbie visited often and Frank never bonded in any meaningful way with John. John never seemed to bond with either of the children but there didn't seem to be any friction between them either.

One night John was with the ham radio club at a campsite where they all gathered to see how many radio contacts they could make with other ham operators all over the world. This was an all-night affair and after watching some TV together, the kids and I had gone to bed. I had left the front door unlocked since I didn't want John to make much noise when he came in. I was just dozing off when I heard the front door open.

"Is that you, John?" I called. No answer, but footsteps were coming down the hall.

"Is that you, Robbie?" I urgently inquired. By this time I was getting a very uneasy feeling. No answer. Footsteps still were coming down the hall.

Frank had gotten a BB gun for Christmas. I yelled. "Frank, do you have your rifle?"

"Yes, ma'am," he said.

"Then shoot that son of a bitch in our hall," I yelled.

"Yes, ma'am!" Frank yelled back.

I heard the footsteps run the other way and the front door slam as our intruder left the premises, post haste. Frank joined me in the hall and we looked out the front window and did not see anyone. We made some hot chocolate and watched some late night TV together. Bonded by our narrow escape but feeling that the two of us had stood together and faced a bad situation and won. We were happy and content and fell asleep on the couch with the TV running. John found us on the couch when he came in around four o'clock that morning. We all laughed together and congratulated Frank on his quick thinking. After all he did have a really high IQ.

Life was easy if a little boring. I worked, studied, attended college. John worked for Bell South and did his ham radio for fun. The kids went to school, played with the neighborhood children, and brought home a Siamese cat that we named Tinker Bell.

Chapter 34: The Snow Storm

In Warner Robins, Georgia, snow is a big event. If one flake falls every person in town stops what they are doing and runs outside to watch. The most we ever have is a light dusting that you might make into a tiny ball, roll across the yard, and gather every little bit up along with the grass and make a snowman of three-inch balls that melt before you can take a picture of it.

One February day in 1973, a snowflake fell and then another and as everyone gathered outside to watch, it kept coming down. And kept coming down. And kept coming down. Warner Robins, Georgia, got thirteen inches of snow followed by three days of weather cold enough to keep it from melting. Everything came to a standstill except the fun. There were no snowplows, no large bags of salt, no snow shovels. Cars could not move, so no one could go to work or the grocery store or anywhere else. On the second day of frozen wonder, my wonderful son Frank had his fourteenth birthday. We built a snowman, shared cake with all the neighborhood, and hurried back inside to tell stories. There are no winter coats in Georgia that withstand below freezing temperatures for more than an hour or two. Though some people were tiring of the snow by the third day when it began to melt, it had remained pristine, since there was no traffic. When it began to melt it was gone in a few hours except where it had piled up. But the sense of magic stayed for days. I have always considered it the perfect gift for Frank on his birthday.

Snow melted, life went back to normal. Colleene, my daughter, made friends with the girl next door and Karen spent more time at our house than her own, which was full of boys. She had three older brothers and I think they thought of her as their slave.

One day Colleene asked me to let Karen spend the night. I told her that she knew I didn't allow anyone to spend the night with her on a school night. She shrugged and left the room. When she was in the other room, I overheard her say "I told you she would not let you spend the night on a school night."

Karen said "You could beg her."

Colleene answered, "You don't know my mom at all. She never gives in to begging. When she says no, she means no." It sounded kind of harsh but I was proud of that reputation. She did not sound offended. It seemed like she liked to know that I would stand my ground if she needed me and that was okay with her.

Tinker Bell, our beloved Siamese, did not like the snow. She would put her paw in it, shake it daintily, lick it off, and back up to the door to be let back in. Later that summer new next-door neighbors moved in. They had a big German Shepherd dog. On cool mornings you could see Tinker Bell lying close to the big dog keeping warm. She considered it okay to visit next door when she was cold, but the dog was not allowed in Tinker Bell's territory. The instant the dog stepped into our yard Tinker Bell hissed and got her hair all standing up and the poor dog yelped and returned to his yard. Then the next cold morning you would see Tinker Bell snuggled up to him again. A strange friendship not unlike many of the human friendships I have known.

Karen's brothers brought home a St. Bernard, a huge St. Bernard that often wandered into our back yard. Tinker Bell didn't like that intrusion. One day Tinker Bell was outside in the back yard when the St. Bernard came to visit. The next thing we knew the St. Bernard was running down the street howling loud enough to bring out all the neighbors. When he came back in sight, we were astounded to see Tinker Bell riding on his head with her claws attached to his nose. Everyone howled with laughter. We stopped him, gathered Tinker Bell, and returned inside the house. We never had another visit from the St. Bernard.

The strangest phenomena with Tinker Bell was her total dislike of my brother, Keith. Whenever he entered the house, she would hiss at him and go hide, unless she was on top of the refrigerator, one of her favorite perches. If he walked by while she was there, she would leap onto his head and dig in her claws. Keith became very wary of walking by my refrigerator. Many years later I would come to understand the enmity she felt for him. It seemed really strange at the time. Keith was the only person she ever attacked.

Life went on. Frank sang in the chorus at school. Colleene struggled with school and repeated the fourth grade to improve her ability to read. In her second run at fourth grade, she ran away from home. Coming home from work one day I found a tear-stained note from her that said she could not cause me to lose my job so she was running away. I searched all of the neighborhood and checked with her friends, but no one had seen her. Just as I was walking in the door, not knowing where else to look the phone rang. It was my mother. She had just found Colleene hiding in her back yard. I immediately got in the car and rushed over. When I saw Colleene she ran to me and cried, "I can't always be good in school and I don't want you to lose your job."

"What are you talking about?" I asked as I pulled her onto my lap.

"My teacher says that if I don't behave in class, she will make sure you get fired from your job."

Of course, I did not believe this so I made an appointment to see her teacher the next afternoon after school. Houston County had just integrated that year and Colleene had one of the black teachers that had been transferred from a formerly all black school to a formerly all-white school. I heartily approved of this change. Having lived outside the south I felt that we in the south needed to move away from our old ways and make more of an effort to treat everyone equally. When I sat down with Colleene's teacher, I looked around the room. There were spitballs on the ceiling and wads of paper on the floor and the room was in total chaos.

The teacher asked what I needed to talk to her about. I said that Colleene had told me that she was afraid I would lose my job if she misbehaved in class and I knew she must have somehow misunderstood. The teacher began shaking her head with a really sad kind of look.

"I just don't know what to do," she said. "These kids don't mind me at all. When I taught at my old school last year, I didn't have this kind of problem. The kids were always respectful to their teachers.

If they misbehaved, either I spanked them or the principal spanked them. This school doesn't believe in spanking children. You can look at this room and see I can't get them under control. So I try anything I can think of to get them to behave. One thing that seems to work is when I threaten to get their parents fired from their jobs. "

I sat there a moment in disbelief. Then said gently "Well, Colleene ran away from home so I wouldn't get fired, I don't think you should tell lies and scare my daughter like that."

"What can I do?" she asked seeming to really be asking for advice. I really didn't know what to tell her and suddenly I felt very sorry for her caught in this transition with everything so different.

When I left her, I went to the principal and explained to him why I was there. He told me he didn't know what to do either. So I just told Colleene to be kind to her teacher, that all this change was very hard for her teacher and if I heard that she misbehaved in class I would personally see she got a spanking, but I would not be losing my job over anything she did in class. I didn't hear any more about any troubles in school. I didn't know if Colleene was better in class or if I just was not being told about it.

I was working, going to college at night, cooking, cleaning, and mothering and in general staying extra busy. Something seemed wrong in our house but I just thought it was normal ups and downs. John worked, the kids went to school, had friends, had fights, argued and made up. Just normal daily life.

Chapter 35: Education

For me, education was lifeblood. I hungered for that "aha" moment when something suddenly made sense, when a new piece of information filled the void in my basic understanding of the universe. I loved the sense of awe when I discovered something totally unthought of before in my mind. It was what sent me back to high school when I was a widow of twenty-one and it drove me to college courses provided at night by Robins Air Force Base when I began work there as a secretary.

I had fallen in love with crossword puzzles when I had left school to become a mother and wife. I loved learning new words and meanings. These little puzzles had kept alive that sense of learning something new each day. I loved reading in the same way. In Bermuda there was a shed behind the house that we rented and I found books that I devoured with a hunger that previously had been satisfied with the library in Warner Robins. One book was about a man who after marrying discovered he liked to dress as a woman. I don't remember the name of the book, but as I read about his struggle to understand himself, I searched my own self and life and wondered if some of my unhappiness in my marriage was because of some part of me that was not content with marriage to a man. I had no desire for a woman but I knew a deep discontent in my life in this marriage with my two small children and a husband who I didn't always approve of and who no longer wooed me with his charm. I put this thought away, took a night course in accounting, and was satisfied for a while with the excitement of learning a new way of looking at numbers. Frank's jealousy put a stop to my night school and I was again, not unhappy, but discontented with my life.

Now, with John, I was married again. Life was routine: work, home, children, cleaning, etc. I wanted something more and college at night filled part of that void. One of my first courses was an English course that required us to read classic literature like "Tess of the d'Urbervilles" by Thomas Hardy and "Wuthering Heights." These were much more difficult reading than the novels I had read voraciously while living in Massachusetts and Bermuda, but I loved the challenges to my understanding and the expansion of my world to include other times, other places. I remember we were to write a few paragraphs or a poem about water in class. In high school I had garnered a lot of praise for my attempts at poetry, so I proudly wrote a poem about water in its many phases, ice, oceans, rain, etc. My little bubble burst when I received the paper back with "The paucity of your vocabulary is appalling" written across it in big red handwriting. I had to look up "paucity" in the dictionary, which I felt proved her point. But that note opened a door that I had kept tightly closed for a long time. Whenever I used a word my mother did not know, she always replied angrily that it was rude and unkind to use words people did not understand. Suddenly one word from an English professor allowed me to use the words I had learned in my crossword puzzles and my reading. On my next essay in that class, she had me read my essay out loud to the class as an example of clear use of opening sentence, paragraph structure, and use of vocabulary. This is why I loved education. I could learn and grow and as I grew, be appreciated in that growth.

I found that same satisfaction in learning Economics, Statistics, Biology, and each of the other subjects I was taking in my night courses. I was proud to be good at being a secretary. I was proud to be a good cook. My children seemed healthy and happy and my husband, John, did not seem to mind my being away at classes at night.

So, we continued this pattern. After eight years of attending night classes, I had completed two years of course work on my Bachelor of Arts degree. I had been promoted twice as a secretary. I had taken a test to get on a training program for Program Management type jobs. I was told by the psychologist in charge of that testing that I had made one of the highest scores on the base, but that the "powers that be" had determined that clerical personnel were not qualified for these positions. My brother who was working on the flight line as a packaging specialist qualified with his much lower grade. I became unsettled with my work as a secretary, I wanted more of a challenge. I decided to quit work and go to college full time. I would become a teacher. Our finances were in a position that I could afford the tuition and our car would be paid off in a month. Once the car was paid off, we could easily live on John's salary for two years and I had enough savings to pay for the tuition. John said he thought he should go to college first. I waited one year. He had not signed up for any college courses or made any attempt to get started, so I put my foot down, quit my job, and enrolled full time at Middle Georgia College in Cochran, Georgia. Oh, what a glorious day. By this time, I was thirty years old, but I had gone to high school at twenty-one, so being thirty in college was no hindrance at all. Life was good.

At this time Georgia colleges were on a quarter system. I spent one quarter at Middle Georgia College and realized that I was bored. In each class we were given a reading assignment each Friday with questions to answer from the assignment. On Monday and Tuesday we discussed the reading material and the questions. On Wednesday we had a test and anyone who made an A on the test would attend class on Thursday, which was a review of the test, and then be exempt from the second test on Friday. But, as a student, you had to be on campus on Friday even if you were exempt from the tests. The professors were excellent, but I studied the questions, read the material, and usually made in the upper ninetieth percentile on Wednesdays. I was bored out of my mind on Thursdays and Fridays. I had to rethink where I wanted to go to college.

Mercer University, in Macon, Georgia, was a private college and about twice as expensive as Middle Georgia College. I read all of the material and decided that I really wanted to go to Mercer. The tuition, though more expensive, was still within the range of my savings, so I applied and was accepted at Mercer for the next quarter. And wonder of all wonders, they transferred all of my credits from the night school and Middle Georgia College. I had been told that Mercer was a very tough school and that they often did not accept grades from other schools. When I asked why they had accepted all of my courses, the counselor said that my grades were high enough to qualify for transfer. What a difference classes were at Mercer. I had to study hard, concentrate completely, and struggle in some classes to keep up. It was exhilarating. At that time Mercer had no classes on Wednesdays, but the professors were there to help anyone struggling. I kept my biology and statistics teachers busy most Wednesdays. I loved it. And most amazing of all, the students were friendly and I never had to pass time in the student union between classes alone.

In March of 1975, I finished all my course work and graduated with a Bachelor of Arts degree with a major in English and a minor in Art. I qualified as a high school teacher in English with the ability to teach Art at least two classes each day.

Chapter 36: Just Day to Day

While I was attending classes at night at Robins AFB, things at home were more or less static. John didn't seem to mind me being gone two nights a week and the children seemed not to bother him while he played with his ham radio which filled the closet in the den.

There was little romance in my life, but I was doing well in school. I had been promoted at work and now was the secretary in an office at the Air Force Reserve building. I worked for three men who were very pleased with my work. They traveled around to inspect the Air Force Reserve units and at each place brought back goodies for me. From the Milwaukee base they brought back excellent cheeses and from the New Orleans base they brought back big burlap bags full of fresh oysters. We took turns having everyone and their spouses over for a big cookout with the oysters. I had never tasted raw oysters before and quickly learned to love them on crackers with horseradish and catsup. We had them cooked on the grill wrapped in seaweed, oyster stew, and raw. I loved all of their wives and we all became friends.

John still ate his oatmeal in bed in the morning. He was so not a morning person that it made life easier for me and the kids if he stayed in bed while we ate breakfast. One morning I had opened a new pack of instant oatmeal and taken it to him in bed, then gone into the kitchen and eaten with the children. When I walked back into the bedroom to get dressed, John was furious.

"You think you are so funny don't you?" he yelled.

"What are you talking about?" I said.

"Putting salt in my oatmeal instead of sugar is not funny" he growled.

"I did not put salt in your oatmeal. I don't know what you are talking about" I said as I gathered up his full bowl of oatmeal and started out of the room.

"You think you are a good cook and you can't even make instant oatmeal," he taunted.

Without thinking about it, I turned around with that full bowl of oatmeal and walked over to the bed and dumped the whole bowl over his head. Then self -preservation kicked in. I took off running. He was close behind with oatmeal spattering everywhere as we ran through the kitchen and the rest of the house. Then I ran back to the bedroom and curled up on the bed so he could only hit my back. He punched me on the arm and them stomped into the bathroom to take a bath. We avoided each other as we dressed and he left in a huff.

As soon as he left, I called my daddy. "John hit me," I whimpered.

"Why did he hit you?" daddy asked, seemingly ready to come to my defense but wanting to know the whole story before he committed himself.

"Well," I stumbled, "I poured a bowl of oatmeal over his head."

I could hear daddy stifling a laugh. "I guess he sorta of had a right then, don't you, Pennywinkle?"

At that, we both began laughing and I knew everything was going to be okay. I told daddy the whole story and he said he was proud of me for standing up for myself but you really couldn't blame John for hitting me on the arm. I agreed and finished the conversation feeling okay and a little giggly. I got dressed and went in to work a little late.

After being at work about an hour, John called. "You will never guess what just happened to me," he said. "I was in the bathroom and one of the guys asked me what was in my ear. When I felt in my ear, I pulled out a blob of oatmeal. I didn't know what to tell him. So, I just told him the whole story and everyone here is laughing and laughing." We laughed together and it seemed everything was okay again. We did, however, continue to find blobs of oatmeal in the oddest of places for the next few years. I once opened a camera cover several years later and for a moment didn't know what that grayish blob was that fell out until I looked closer and burst out laughing. Life went back to its old routine. Work, kids, school, lessons, cooking, and cleaning.

A friend of mine started coming over a lot. She was going through a divorce and needed a lot of comforting. I tried to be a friend and listen to her troubles but I needed to study and keep up with a lot of my other duties, so sometimes while I was cooking or cleaning she talked to John as I did whatever I needed to do to keep things going.

I began to feel like she was a drama queen and a nuisance there all the time, but I tried to be sympathetic and kind as a friend should be in another's time of trouble. She started coming over on the nights I was away at school and one night I came in and John was holding her against his chest patting her on the back. Jealously kicked in. I told her she needed to go because we needed our sleep and she left still crying. Then I turned on John, "I don't think it is appropriate for her to be here while I am gone," I said.

"We weren't doing anything," he answered defensively.

I dropped it but I knew I had a plan to stop this. The next day I called her and told her I didn't think she should come over while I wasn't there. She agreed that if it made me uncomfortable, she would not come over when I was away at school.

The next couple of weeks we talked on the phone a couple of times, but she did not come over at all. Then I came home a little early from class one night and there she was sitting really close to him and as though they had been holding each other before I walked in. I was devastated. She quickly left. John was silent. I was so furious; I just stomped into the bedroom and went to bed. I don't know what time he came to bed, but he stayed on his ham radio until I had gone to sleep.

The next morning, we were civil but we did not discuss it. He did not apologize or make excuses. I went to work, asked for some vacation time and came home and packed the kids up and left John a note that I was going to visit his mother.

I could not believe what a beautiful trip the kids and I had driving to New Jersey. In Tennessee we saw a sign for a Daniel Boone restaurant. A show about Daniel Boone was on TV at that time and Frank really wanted to go to that restaurant. We stopped at a little log cabin with a small sign out front that said Daniel Boone slept here. We had a big southern breakfast with waffles, biscuits, eggs, bacon, and sausage with grits. To this day Frank remembers that wonderful breakfast we had that day in that unexpected little restaurant in the middle of nowhere.

That trip became an adventure. We would drive a while and then explore. We went looking for exotic restaurants to eat in and we laughed and told jokes as we drove. So different from our trips with John driving where everyone was quiet and we were trying to beat some inner goal he had set to get there as soon as possible.

After spending the night in a motel with a pool and enjoying watching the kids so totally relaxed, we arrived at Mrs. Burdge's house in Asbury Park, New Jersey. She was expecting me, but was curious why John was not with us. At first, I just told her he couldn't get off from work but would be up later. Then, over a glass or two of wine, I told her the whole story and said I needed to get away to figure out where to go from there. She was so comforting. She agreed that I needed more options before I made a decision. We decided that we would go bar hopping the next day after she got off from work. Frannie and Georgianna (John's sisters) would be there with the kids and we could have the whole night to relax and regroup.

Anne Marie (Mrs. Burdge) worked at a brewery and since she was single, she was accustomed to going to a bar after work each day with some of her co-workers and friends. I met her at the bar and could not believe it when she introduced me as a friend of hers who was visiting from Florida where I was a model. I had never felt so beautiful or cared for. I couldn't believe the guys really bought into me being a model and drooled over me the whole time we were there. When I asked her why she had told them I was a model. She said "If John doesn't appreciate you, we can find someone who will." Again, I had found a defender in the most unexpected place and I savored it.

Around seven o'clock, we left the bar and went to a little house to eat. She told me it was owned by the mafia and you had to be known to get in. It was small and cozy and the food was amazing. There was a little old lady in the kitchen who had pastas and sauces on the stove and talked to you about what she could fix you. There were only seven or eight tables set up in the living and dining room of the house and you felt like you were family when you went there.

After three days of being cherished by Anne Marie, John flew in and we picked him up at the airport. He apologized about my friend and agreed I had every right to leave him if I wanted to, but he hoped I would stay and he would not see her when I wasn't there. I was so glad it was resolved. We visited with his family for a few days and returned home to settle back into our routine of home, school, work, kids, ham radio and him eating oatmeal in bed each day while the kids and I enjoyed our breakfast in peace.

Chapter 37: A New Career

Mercer University was amazing. I majored in English and minored in Art and Education. I loved Art the most but knew careers in art were very iffy. Since English was a required subject in all high schools and I really wanted to be a teacher, English was the most logical course of action and, let's face it, I loved English, too. I loved writing, reading, and talking; especially talking. What other course of action was there? I was in my junior year at college and only had to take two science courses, a Philosophy course, and a Statistics course, and all my required course curriculum was completed. I could fill all the rest of my time on Art, English, and Education classes. I gloried in Chaucer, Shakespeare, and the Romantic period; Composition, Printing, Pottery, Weaving, and Painting. The education classes included working one quarter in a school that had policemen in the corridors and the teachers had safety pins in their drawers to pass out when girls came to school with no bras and buttons missing from their blouses. Once we went on a field trip with a class and a boy about twelve asked me if I wanted to fuck with him. I was flabbergasted. Where did a child this young learn such language and how to use it? Did he really want to shock me or did he think it was cute? It was quite an eye opener for this Georgia cracker who has never attended a school other than those where the majority were middle class and, to my knowledge, most had never gone hungry or lacked for the necessities of life.

Next, I spent some time with a school for children with disabilities. I was assigned a child who was about five years old and who sat docilely and clapped her hands all day. She did not interact with anyone and my teacher and I worked out a plan to use positive reinforcement to get a response from her. Each day I brought cookies and said, "have a cookie" as I moved them further and further out of her reach. By the end of two weeks, we felt we had reached a major goal: she got up out of her chair and came three steps to the table to get a cookie. The next day when I went back, the teacher in charge of the class told me she could no longer use me. It seems little Caroline had gotten out of her chair at home to get something from the table and her parents were irate. As long as she never got out of her chair, they did not have to watch her to protect her. They knew they could go about their business and she would stay in her chair, but now she was moving on her own about the house and they felt she was a danger to herself and others. I sadly left the school wondering what I would have done in her parent's shoes.

The next quarter I did my full-time student teaching at my old high school, Northside High in Warner Robins. My supervising teacher was Brenda Littlefield. What a wonderful mentor she was. The quarter I was there she was teaching Shakespeare. When I was in high school, Shakespeare was a boring class. Our teacher had chosen Julius Caesar as the play we studied. Brenda made Shakespeare come alive and the students loved her and Shakespeare. We studied "A Midsummer Night's Dream," a play that could entertain any teenager. After a few weeks she turned over one class a day to me. Under her tutelage, I was able to keep her high standards of being tough but making it exciting. All my dreams of being a teacher were realized and I fell in love with the fact that I was going to be a teacher.

My last quarter of college was done. I finished all of my required subjects for both graduation and a teaching certificate with a major in English. It was March and graduation ceremonies were not until June but that did not deter me. I talked to Brenda and she arranged an interview with the Superintendent of Houston County Schools. The next day I got a call from the Principal of Warner Robins High School, Mr. Smith. We set up an interview.

I did not realize how influential Brenda Littlefield was until I was interviewed by Mr. Smith, the principal. He had an English teacher that was leaving and needed a teacher to finish out the year. That interview was the strangest interview I have ever had. It seemed that he was trying to convince me to come to work for him instead of having me tell him why I thought I was qualified for the job. I accepted. On the next Monday I began teaching at Warner Robins High School, the current teacher, Mrs. Burch, was leaving at the end of the week and we had one week of her showing me the ropes of her classes. It was under the quarter system at that time and I inherited classes that included "Beowulf" and creative writing. Since I was following a very creative teacher that the students loved whose name was Burch and I was Mrs. Burdge, I had no trouble assimilating into her schedule. How lucky was I to have good friends and to have achieved my goal of teaching. The world was my oyster.

Chapter 38: Teaching and Changes

Over the summer we did a lot of changes in our lifestyle. I was now earning money again and we could afford a bigger house. So we bought a beautiful ranch style house with a sloping back yard filled with trees. We moved in and began to feel richer and more fulfilled. John now had a closet in the den for his ham radio and we all had bigger bedrooms. John spent a lot of time on his radio and I happily did lesson plans and cooked in my new larger kitchen. I had always enjoyed cooking and now I had a little more money to experiment and try new recipes. John ate to stop hunger. He did not care what he ate and at times that was truly disappointing. However, my beautiful son Frank enjoyed my adventures in the culinary arts and he started planning and cooking one meal a week. Our enjoyment of finding and trying new recipes spilled over into other parts of our lives. Once in his pediatrician's waiting room we were comparing recipes in the ladies' magazines and the nurse teased us that maybe it was time for Frank to move on up to a doctor for adults. His pediatrician, Dr. English, agreed so we reluctantly made our next appointment for Frank at a doctor that did not specialize in children's illnesses. At 6'3, Frank was definitely adult sized.

I once found a recipe for lobster thermidor and planned to surprise John when he came home from work with this elegant dish. When he came in, I told him I had a special treat for him but it wouldn't be ready for about fifteen minutes. He said he was hungry right then and made himself a peanut butter sandwich and went into his ham radio closet and would not come out for dinner. I called my brother, Robbie, and he rushed over. We had a feast and a joyous dinner without John. Somehow the fact that John did not care did not dissuade me from continuing my love of cooking and new explorations of different recipes.

When the fall quarter started at school I was surprised and pleased that I had been assigned two art classes, one creative writing class, one American Literature class, and a class called CVAE (Career Vocational Associative Education). When I asked what CVAE was, I was informed by the other teachers with a roll of their eyes that my class was the English portion of a half-day curriculum for students that were on parole from the juvenile detention center and that the best I could do would be to keep those students in order for the forty-five minutes I had with them each day. My class was just before lunch and their last class of the day as they worked in the afternoons at jobs assigned them by the parole board. I thought they probably gave me the art classes and the creative writing class to compensate for what they considered a punishing class of students that nobody else wanted.

I jumped into the classes with enthusiasm and had a lot to learn. Following in Mrs. Burch's shoes the year before had been an easy task. She had already set the pace and provided me with her lesson plans for the rest of the quarter. On my own now, I could choose how to approach each class. The textbooks were guides but I had a lot of freedom on what kind of activities I would use to pique the students' interest and still give them all the information that needed to take from my classes to have a more educated view of life.

The CVAE students and classes were the biggest challenge. All the CVAE teachers met regularly and had no set curriculum for how to address these students' needs. I decided first to assess where my students were in their reading and writing skills and was appalled that I had two students who could not read. I asked the other CVAE teachers how they addressed this and they said that it was not a problem. These two students would not disturb the class if they were assigned a page or two of the textbook to copy. When I looked at their copied text, I realized that they were dyslexic. They reversed letters in words they copied. I was at a loss how to address this and talked to the school counselor and she said that since they were in the tenth grade there was little we could do now. I noticed that the other students treated these two students as though they were dumb and I thought this was not the case. I decided the best way to check this out was to determine how good their memory was. So I decided to play the game "I am going on a trip" with the class. In this game you begin with the first person in the row and they start with "I am going on a trip and I am taking…" wherein they choose any object they would like to take on a trip. The next person says "I am going on a trip and taking…" whatever the first person said and they add and item they would like to take to the first person's item, etc. My first dyslexic student was fourth in line and surprised everyone when she easily remembered the other three items and gleefully added her own item with no problem. However, my second dyslexic student was fifteenth and the class said "Oh, you can just skip him, there is no way he can remember all the items." I asked him did he want to try and he grinned really big and started. He pointed to each person and enumerated the item they had chosen and when he reached himself, he gleefully added his own item. There was total silence for a moment, then everyone cheered and started patting him on the back. After allowing this to go on for a little, I got the class back in order and we finished the game just as the bell rang. I watched the rest of the year as the class assimilated these two students who had formerly been shunned into their clique. Even though they were outsiders to the rest of the school all of the CVAE class was now included in their own little family.

I taught them how to read advertisements in newspapers and shop for bargains, how to calculate how much interest cost them when they bought on credit, how to balance a checkbook and write a check, and in anatomy we compared a horse's anatomy to the human ones they were studying in science class. Then I took them to a stable and gave them all the opportunity to ride a horse. They worked hard for me and I adored them.

Once a new student joined the class on a day we were taking a test. I gave him a copy of the test and told him to please take the test, that he would not be graded on it but it would give me some insight into what we would need to do to catch him up to where the rest of the class was. He wadded up the test and threw it on the floor. I told him to put his head down on the desk and sleep or go to the office. He slept. The next day he was not in class. I checked with the office to see if they knew where he was and was told that he got in a fight in the parking lot after school the day before and was pretty bruised up and would probably be out for a couple of days. When he came back, he was very respectful. The word came drifting back to me that some of the students had said to him "You disrespected our teacher and we don't put up with that." I never got it firsthand but it made me feel that my efforts were appreciated. The other teachers did not understand it but were glad that I volunteered to keep that class the whole time I taught there.

Chapter 39: Teaching

We were under the quarter system at school and the second quarter of my first year, the school added Science Fiction and the Supernatural to the curriculum. I jumped at the opportunity to teach that class. There were so many ways to go with the class. We started with Poe and some of the early writers and progressed to Heinlein. I always aimed to reach the reluctant students and wished only to teach each student to love reading. My theory has always been that reading anything is an education unto itself and if a person likes to read, they will never stop learning. In my zeal to make reading fun I bored some of the best students. In the science fiction class we had ghost story Fridays once a month. Almost every family has its own ghost stories and those Fridays became a favorite with the class. Once just as the bell rang for class to start on a cloudy rainy day, the lights went off in my class and the students came in humming, carrying lit candles and a casket. I was so pleased. The ghost stories that day were especially haunting.

Art class began as a real challenge. The whole football team had signed up for the class. When they signed up, I had given each student a supply list and told them that if they couldn't afford the supplies to let me know. No one had come to me with a problem so I began my first class with a drawing lesson. The football team came to the class and did not have their supplies. When I asked why, they informed me that they were the football team and the art class was a class they took to relax and that Mr. Gupton always let them go outside and paint garbage cans or whatever. They were not required to participate in the art class. I informed them that it was an "art" class and they would have supplies and participate or get zeroes for each day they did not have supplies or take part in the class.

By the end of the day, I had been summoned to the principal's office. "You are not to require the football players to do art. You know they are not going to be any good at it and we have a school policy that they have to maintain a certain grade average to stay on the team," he informed me.

"Then you need to get them to bring their supplies and do art. I am teaching an art class. I am not babysitting a football team," I said. "If they do their best, they will make good grades. I don't grade art on proficiency, only endeavor."

He studied me for a few minutes before dismissing me. The next day all of the football players had the appropriate supplies and grudgingly participated in the class. Gradually their attitude changed. They enjoyed the class and sometimes exclaimed, "Wow, I did it and it doesn't look bad." Because they had big, muscled hands, the artwork was often squared off and bulky but gorgeous. Some were making A's and I heard them say that I was giving them good grades because they were football players. I went to the library and found books with African art and brought them to class. They were amazed at how closely their work resembled some of the work in the books and said, "You weren't just giving us A's. You really thought our work was as good as this?" to which I just smiled. I loved watching them grow after that and some of them became really good artists in addition to being good athletes.

Things at home were not quite right. Frank spent more time in his room with the door closed and Colleene became angry all the time. Her attitude at school was bad and she got in fights. Once she was sent for one week to detention school which was used to keep from expelling students. It was very strictly run by a retired Air Force Sergeant. When I asked what the fight was about, nobody was talking. This year Frank came over and we were talking about my stories and he asked me was I going to tell about Colleene and the fight. I told him I didn't know what the fight was about so I might just mention it as part of the rising rift between Colleene and me. He looked at me funny, then you could see him making a decision to tell me something that he had known a long time and finally felt I had a right to know.

"She was in the back hall with the smokers and going on and on about what a bad person you are. One of the football players told her to stop dissing you. She laughed and said, "Make me!" turned and started laughing about how bad you were. He grabbed her and told her to stop. She hit him and he pushed her and walked away. One of the other students reported it to the principal and he decided to just tell everyone she started a fight and leave it at that."

This story saddened me. I knew that Colleene and I were having problems, but did not know the whole school knew it, too. Shortly after that incident, I found a therapist for her and within a few months she left home to go live with a boy she had met who was from Macon. They married a few months later. When I talked to the therapist about it, he told me to let her go because she was very unhappy at home and maybe she could find a better place in another environment. I made peace with her and we held the wedding at our house.

Chapter 40: Teaching 3

After the first year of teaching art, the principal, Mr. Smith, asked me would I like to teach three classes of art. In order to teach three classes of any subject you had to have a teaching certificate in that subject. Since I had only minored in art in college, I did not have enough art credits to get an art teaching certificate. We discussed that and he said that if I could get the credits I needed to get the art teaching certificate over the summer the school board would pay for the courses. I was thrilled. I called Mr. Hutto, my art teacher at Mercer, and asked him was it possible for me to complete three art courses over the summer. He said, "We will make it work." He managed to figure out a way where most of my work was done independently with his supervision over the summer. Due to his help and my hard work, by fall quarter I had teaching certificates in English and Art.

I added a pottery course to the curriculum at Warner Robins High School. I think I got the whole football team and half of my Creative Writing class in that one classroom. What a wild ride. Clay was a great medium for the large hands of the football players and my creative writing students loved making the most fantastic vases with skulls, snakes, and dragons. Some of them made the tops of the vases fit over their mouth and had little side spouts. I pretended that I did not know that these were really "bongs" for smoking pot because they were pretty amazing artworks and I wanted them to be as creative as possible. I think that somehow left the impression that I smoked pot myself. One day one of the students came in and offered me "some really good weed." I quickly told him I knew he was kidding. He quickly replied that "No, It is really good stuff."

I told him if he wasn't kidding I would have to report him to the office and he might be arrested. He replied, "Oh, no ma'am, it is the best stuff you can find."

I reported him to the office and he was tried and sent to juvenile detention. Years later I ran into him at a party and he said he remembered me as the teacher that turned him in. I told him he gave me no choice. He laughed and said, "that was some really good stuff and I had already had a lot of it when I came to class that day." I was relieved that he did not feel he had left me a choice.

I was so proud of my creative writing class and my art class that I convinced another teacher to help me put together a magazine each quarter featuring my creative writing student's work illustrated by my art students. It was fabulous. Everyone loved it. The students proudly sold it to everyone they could get to buy it and we all took the money and went to Six Flags over Georgia one Saturday. We laughed and they began singing songs while they waited in line for the rides. It was a beautiful sunshiny day and we all climbed in the van exhausted and happy after the fireworks at dark. Each quarter we worked hard on putting it together and selling it and then each class chose their own way of celebrating. One went to the stables where I had a horse. One just chose to go on a picnic by the river and swim. They were all so creative and each outing had its own special feeling.

Gradually I became disillusioned with teaching. I loved teaching, but I began to hate the regulations imposed on us. The school board decided to mainstream the children with behavioral disorders. They felt art class was a good place to start. I understood the need to mainstream but when you place two or three students with behavior problems in an art class you create havoc. My art classes were very unstructured. We worked on a particular medium such as clay or painting but each student was allowed to choose what they wanted to paint or sculpt and I walked around the room and helped each student individually. These new students were problematic. They could not concentrate and stay in their seats and work. They wandered the room and sometimes destroyed other students works. In one of the classes there was a very tall strong young man who constantly wanted my full attention. He would grab my arm while I was helping another student and no matter how many times I asked him to sit down, he did not stay sitting for more than a minute. He also grabbed my arm with a strength that I am sure he did not realize was bruising my arm. One day one of the football players noticed the bruises on my arm and asked me where they were coming from. I told him that Hightower did not know his own strength and the bruises were where he grabbed me, but it was okay they did not hurt much. The rest of the quarter that Hightower was in my class, he never touched me again. I asked about it, having learned from my CVAE class that the students sometimes overreacted to anyone harming me. One of the girls assured me that the football players had just talked to him.

The other teachers began to avoid me. I got a reputation for letting the "bad" students get away with stuff in my class and I didn't have much use for teachers who hated teaching and spent all of their time in the teacher's lounge complaining about their students. Then we signed a contract for the next year with a pay raise included in the contract. Before the end of the year the state congress had refused to fund that pay raise and we were told that we would not get the raise that was in the contract. The teachers griped and complained, but no one at our school was willing to fight for it. I was working ten to fifteen hours a day: Five hours of class, grading papers, planning, etc. I was not making a whole lot more than I made on the base as a secretary that was definitely an eight hour a day job. The college professors in Georgia decided that they would sign each check as partial payment of the contractual sum and sue for the amount listed on their contract, but the teachers at my school would not agree to do that. My son was graduating that year so I applied for a job on the base that was a training position where I would start at just a few dollars less that I was making in the school system and guaranteed a promotion each year for three years. I would almost double my salary in the three years. I was accepted on the base and left my job as a teacher at the end of that school year.

It was three years of learning and growing and a lot of stories that still fill me with joy. It filled me with joy and a sense of self that was much stronger than before, but I looked forward to my new adventure with excitement.

Chapter 41: Horses

When Colleene was fourteen and I had started teaching, we had more spendable income and since she had always said she wanted to ride horses, I found a stable on the base that had horses available for young riders to learn how to ride. So, for over a year, I took her on most Saturday mornings to the stable and dropped her off. She always seemed excited to go riding and was much easier to deal with at home. As Christmas neared, I got so excited about finally knowing for sure what I could buy for her that would make her ecstatic. I had a friend from grade school, Pat Dickson, whose father had retired from the base and started raising horses. When I contacted him, he assured me he had a gentle horse she would love. Charlie, the horse, was a very small gentle horse that followed Mr. Dickson around like a pet dog. I fell in love with the idea of surprising Colleene with this wonderful, sweet horse. Mr. Dickson gave me a list of the equipment I would need and the name of a stable where he could be boarded. We arranged to have Charlie gelded early enough that he would be healed by Christmas, bought a saddle and harness, and moved him to his new stable a few days before Christmas so he could settle in, and awaited the great day.

Christmas day dawned; a beautiful sunny day with mild temperatures. Colleene opened the saddle and went berserk with excitement, jumping around and giggling. We grabbed a bite to eat and headed for the stable. The man who ran the stable, Rick Goings, met us here and helped her get the saddle, bridle, etc. all in place and secure. She refused any help getting astride her beautiful horse. Off she rode. In my whole life I don't remember being more pleased with a present I had been able to give to another person. The perfect gift. For several weeks we went to the stable every day to feed Charlie. She rode every Saturday and Sunday. Then she began to just go on Saturdays and Sundays. I worried that Charlie was not being properly cared for but, Rick assured me that he fed all the horses in the stable when the owners were too busy, but that we did need to clean the stall at least once a week. I knew Colleene had the stall on the weekends when she rode so I asked him was that a problem. He told me that she had gotten lax and had not cleaned out the stall in a couple of weeks and he had taken care of it, but I either needed to pay more rent to cover the cleaning or get her to do it. I had a talk with her and it seemed to resolve itself.

A few weeks later she called me early from the stable and said she had fallen off the horse and I needed to come and get her. I rushed out there and she declared testily that, "I am fine, I just want to go home."

The next day she said she was sore and it was the day she was supposed to clean the stall and she didn't feel up to it. I commiserated with her and told her not to worry about it, I would take care of cleaning the stall that day.

When I got to the stable Rick was kind and helped me clean the stall and feed the horse. I loved it. He asked me why I didn't come out and ride the horse sometimes. I told him I had never been on a horse and to tell the truth they scared me. He laughed and assured me I would be completely safe and he would love to teach me how to ride.

Over the next few months Colleene went to the stables less and I went more. I loved the sweet gentle Charlie and the way Rick helped me train him. Together we taught Charlie to respond to voice commands and I was taught to control him with the reins, voice, and all the little things that horses respond to like sugar cubes and brushing and kind voices.

John had become more and more distant as I became more independent at work and home and working with this horse felt like I was doing something exciting just for me. Crazy as it sounds, I loved mucking out stalls and spreading new fresh smelling hay in all of the stalls at the stable. I loved working side by side with Rick. Not only was he charming, but he also treated me like I was beautiful and he was drop dead gorgeous. A truly handsome dark eyed Native

American that made my heart beat faster when he smiled at me.

Over time Colleene gradually quit going to the stable altogether. Then she decided she wanted to sell Charlie and spend the money. I laughed at her. Charlie had become mine and that was that. No money. She had given up the right to him when she quit making sure he was fed and comfortable. By caring for him I had become his owner. She pouted but surprisingly let go quickly. I couldn't tell much difference in the anger she had been aiming at me for the last couple of years.

After Colleene abdicated her ownership of Charlie to me, I left school each day, dropped her and Frank at home, and went to the stable. Gradually Rick and I had gone from friendship to lovers. I loved riding out in the woods on Charlie accompanied by this swarthy handsome man and making mad passionate love in the woods or in a newly cleaned stall. We sometimes went to horse shows together and made love in motel rooms. He seemed never to get enough of me and after over ten years with John only wanting sex intermittently and usually at my instigation, I could not get enough of feeling desired, beautiful, and SEXY. AND horseback riding too. What more could a thirty something ask of life?

Rick welcomed my art and creative writing students and gladly showed them how to ride and, those that were afraid to ride, he set up a couple of barrel races for them to watch. The horse owners at the stable gladly participated in these shows. The girls in the classes swooned over Rick and the boys loved the way he treated them like men. I eventually sold my sweet Charlie to one of the men who brought his daughter out every weekend to ride and she always begged to ride Charlie. I bought a fancy racking horse and began to train him and Rick trained me how to ride in racking horse shows. I was way too clumsy on these horses and gladly allowed other people to ride my horse in the shows. As long as I was riding him we never won a blue ribbon, but when an excellent rider rode him in a show we often came home with lots of ribbons. Some of the shows were as far away as Tennessee. Rick had a horse trailer and we got away for whole weekends together, sometimes just us, but most of the time with several other riders from the stable especially when we realized how good the horse was and how well he did with more experienced riders in the saddle. We were very circumspect when there were others along, but when it was just us and no one knew us, we were not so circumspect. I loved feeling beautiful and desired.

Gradually life moved on. I left teaching for a job on the base and John took more trips with AT&T as they changed the technology and he went to other sites to aid in the transition. He was often gone several weeks at a time and I felt at times when he returned that he had slept with someone else. He would say a woman's name in a way that made the hair on my neck kind of prickle. He became more irritable with me and made some disparaging remarks that shocked me. Once when we had ordered fried catfish and I was starving, the catfish arrived so hot that when I put it in my mouth I had to blow in and out really quickly to keep it from burning my tongue. He looked at me and said, "That is disgusting. You eat like a dog." I just stared at him. How could he possibly love me and say such a hurtful thing?

The rift was growing between us and I tried to fix it, but didn't know how. So, I just spent more energy doing a great job at work, enjoying my horse, and enjoying the way Rick made me feel. I also added night school to the mix again. The base would pay my tuition for working on my master's degree at night. They brought in teachers from Georgia College in Milledgeville and two nights a week I spent in class and several nights a week I studied my lessons. My life was full if not quite right. Rick and I gradually grew apart and I sold my racking horse to the mother of a young girl at the stable who had been riding him in the racking horse shows.

Colleene got married. Frank got a basketball scholarship and went off to college. John and I decided to sell the house and move into an apartment in Macon. John became more and more distant and critical of everything I did. Work at the base became a drudge and I was becoming more unhappy. I decided to go to law school. I took the LSAT, made a good score and was accepted into Mercer Law School in Macon. I was excited about a new adventure.

Chapter 42: Stone Mountain

The children had grown up and left the nest. I had grown restless again and left my job on base and applied for law school and been accepted. We had sold our home and moved into an apartment in Macon and I was at a loss for who I was and where I was going.

That summer, before I was supposed to start law school in September, John transferred to Atlanta. We moved to Stone Mountain, Georgia, right outside Atlanta. Law school plans died on the vine and I looked forward to the new adventure of living near Atlanta. I took a job with an Office Temporary Worker service and worked a week or two a month at different places. It was interesting to meet new people and learn to get around in Atlanta. Some of the jobs were tedious and some of the jobs and people I met were really interesting. Some of the people I worked for were exciting and some were just jerks. I remember one place where I refused to work more than one day. The person I worked directly for dictated a letter for me to send to Larry. I asked what address to use and he told me it should be in the secretary's desk somewhere. When I asked what Larry's last name was, he irritably replied that he couldn't do all my work for me. Then when I began typing, the "E" on the typewriter stuck every time I hit it. When I asked him who to call to get the typewriter fixed, he said I was just a lousy typist and I needed to just get that letter typed out. I called the service I worked for and told them I hated leaving them in the lurch but would not finish the day. The placement person whispered that I was not the first one to refuse to work for this gentleman. I felt relieved and picked up my purse, stuck my head in the supervisor's door and said, "I'm not feeling well. I am going home. The temp service will try to find someone else to take my place." I was proud of myself for standing up for myself but I felt a little guilty for leaving the temp service in the lurch. However, it did not affect the way they placed me after that. I was afraid they would not send me on other jobs after that fiasco, but they called me the next day with a placement that lasted for three weeks.

In addition to work, I learned to fill my days with new adventures. One of the ladies in the apartment tried to teach me how to knit. I decided to knit baby booties. Somehow they came out about eight inches long. We laughed and we just talked and laughed while she knitted. A couple of the ladies and I decided that we would try out some of the better restaurants in the area at lunch time. Often really expensive restaurants have very reasonably priced lunches and we took advantage of those lower lunch prices and ate sumptuous meals.

My father's sister, Aunt Helen, lived only a few exits down the interstate from where we were living and she and I took the opportunity of going to the parks and painting "en plein air." She was a wonderful artist and I learned a lot from her. She also introduced me to other artists in the area and brought them to my apartment to show them my work. One of them had some paintings in a gallery and she suggested I see them about hanging some of my work. They took one of my paintings and hung it in their gallery. It was my first time as an adult to really feel accepted as an artist. I loved it.

My mother's sister, Aunt Lucy, also lived nearby and was practically a recluse but she really seemed to enjoy going places with me and I hunted little off the path places to take her. She loved visiting museums and we found several unique little museums that were fascinating. There was a "Gone with the Wind" museum, and a "Stone Mountain Park" museum with a diorama of the battle of Atlanta, there was the art gallery where my picture was hanging and other little places that we visited and laughed. Aunt Lucy was in fragile health and we often had to reschedule our visits based on her health, but each time we did go somewhere together, it was a treat for her and for me.

Stone Mountain also had an animal preserve area where deer and geese roamed and there was a little petting zoo. It always felt peaceful there. I bought a year's membership to Stone Mountain Park and often wandered over the park or took my paints and painted the scenery.

On the 4th of July, the Atlanta Symphony Orchestra held a special concert in the park, with fireworks at the end. John was off on a business trip and I packed a lunch, a blanket and a pillow and went to the park early to get a really good spot on the grass near the stage. I settled in and "people watched" until the Symphony began. I had never heard a live Symphony Orchestra before. When they began playing the William Tell Overture, I was so swept away by the music that tears began to drip down my face. This amazing day opened up a wonderful new avenue of enjoyment for me that has given me so much pleasure for the rest of my life. I love it when life gives you those little unexpected jewels that gleam and bring more glamour and beauty to your whole life.

We only lived in Stone Mountain a little over a year, but it was a year of growth for me and more distancing from John. He spent more time away on business trips, more time in his ham radio closet and once, when I approached him about sex, he said "Oh, okay, Mom said that to be a good husband, I should have sex with my wife at least once a week. So, I guess we can do this now." I was shocked and appalled. Since when had sex become a duty? I spent more and more time with less and less sex. I was not always unhappy. I figured he just had very little sexual drive and that was just the way he was made. So we carried on in a normal way. It is amazing to me now that I did not question what kind of man I was married to that could proclaim he loved me and really not be interested in touching me. But I did accept that he loved me and was just different.

When he transferred back to Macon, we bought a house in Warner Robins with a pool and moved back to a place I felt was truly home. I went back to work as a contracts specialist on the base and another segment of change began.

Chapter 43: Home Again, Home Again, or Not

We settled into a kind of odd routine after moving back to Warner Robins. I guess marriage had become a familiar day to day activity that was not totally satisfying, but not as scary as contemplating a life without it. Colleene now had a son named Philip Dale, called Little Dale, and Frank and his wife Carol had two little girls, Fawna Diane and Angela Renee. I was not a doting grandmother. I did not babysit. I invited the kids over to spend the night and spent time with them on my own schedule.

Each child was very unique. Fawna was creative and my favorite memory of her is when she was tiny and just learning to speak. We sat on the floor pretending to play dress up. I put an imaginary crown on her head and she held her head high and turned it side to side and waved at me. She put imaginary earrings on my ears and I pretended to check them in an imaginary mirror. Then I gave her an imaginary ring and told her it was a nose ring, she immediately placed it on her nostril. I knew she had never seen a nose ring and was tickled that she had put the information together from the name assigned it and had placed this imaginary nose ring in the appropriate place.

Angie was quieter and often liked to help me in the kitchen. They both especially liked playing waitress and bartender. We had a bar set up on the back porch and they loved taking the glasses from the bar and adding ice and bringing me tea and dashes of pretend liquors from bottles with their lids tightly in place. My son once came to pick them up when we were playing this game and was appalled that

I even pretended to drink alcoholic drinks that they had prepared. I told him it was only make believe. He looked hard at me, then grinned sheepishly and said it wouldn't hurt them and they did enjoy playing with me.

Once when Angie was staying with me and she was about four years old, I was marinating some strawberries in cherry liquor in the refrigerator. I had a carton of strawberries in the fruit drawer that were not marinated. Angie and I were watching TV and she asked could she have some strawberries. I said sure and she went into the kitchen and came back with a few strawberries in her hand. I did not think anything about it until she began giggling and twirling around the room. Oh, no, I thought as vision of myself at seven finding my dad's muscadine wine in the fridge and thinking it was grape juice, drinking it, giggling, and twirling just as Angie was now doing flashed through my mind. I quickly grabbed her and asked her to show me where she got the strawberries. She took me to the refrigerator and pointed to the bowl of marinating strawberries and giggled. "I tried both of them and I liked these the best" she slurred slightly. I immediately fixed her a drink of chocolate milk, thinking that might absorb some of the alcohol. She snuggled next to me and went to sleep almost immediately. I didn't think she really knew what had happened until years later she teased me about getting her drunk when she was only four years old.

Little Dale was an entirely different matter. He was defiant about every caution I ever gave him. When the dishwasher door was open, he climbed onto it against my specific instructions. I was bewildered at a three-year-old child with so much rebellion.

They loved the pool and I enjoyed them. I had my children when I was sixteen and seventeen and I did not want the responsibility of raising any more children, but I loved our games and the time we spent together even though I was not a true doting grandmother. So we muddled along forming our own relationships as friendly old granny with a lot of quirks and delightful children, entertaining their granny with silly antics.

Work in contracts at Robins AFB was familiar and almost comfortable. Life with John was familiar and more and more distant. I was not unhappy, but something was missing.

Chapter 44: Changes

Work in the Contracting Department (formally called Procurement) was challenging, but not always nice. The Division Chief was a womanizer and it flowed down to most of the male supervisors. Usually if you were the contracts person on a particular contract and there was a reason to visit the company regarding that contract, the person who wrote the contract visited the off-site company with or without a supervisor. There was a woman in my section who always traveled with the Division Chief on anything to do with my contracts. I loved to travel and resented this, but even worse when that contract had problems and needed to be briefed to the higher ups, I was still required to do the briefing, sometimes without all of the facts that were discussed at the contractor's site. This was very uncomfortable and often put me in the light of a not quite competent contract specialist.

I decided to continue work on my master's degree. The base now had a night program for master's degrees in management. It was free. The only requirement was that your supervisor had to sign a statement that the degree would be relevant to your work. When I asked my supervisor to sign this statement, he told me he would only sign it if I agreed to skip class once in a while and spend some time at night with him. Everything in my life that made me feel small came crashing in on me. I started screaming at him that if he were the last man on earth, I would never meet him after work, and he could just get it into his fat head that if it were the end of the world, I would NEVER sleep with him. Evidently, I was loud enough that the Division Chief, all the way on the other side of the large building heard me and sent his secretary to see what was going on. I got the paper signed. Strangely, nobody moved me to another section, however, my supervisor was very professional with me after that even though when he had to deal with me, he always put his hands in his pockets and jiggled his coins. Nobody ever directly accosted me again. Years later, I had long since left the base, I ran into him in a grocery store and his hands immediately went into his pockets and he began to jingle his coins. I smiled and walked away.

One of the women I worked with in Procurement transferred to Material Maintenance (MM). She told me she loved it and encouraged me to transfer. I put in the paperwork and the transfer went quickly. A new adventure began.

I was put on the Mod Squad. Air Force equipment sometimes needed modifications such as firetrucks being sent to Alaska needed different starting equipment. I was responsible for getting those mods on contract. The people I worked with were a lot more relaxed and I loved that.

During this time John had an affair and confessed it. I told him that I could not throw any stones as I had also had an affair and asked him what he wanted to do. He assured me he loved me and wanted to stay married. I was not really surprised by his confession. He was away from home a lot as AT&T had taken over Southern Bell and a lot of changes in equipment were going into effect. John was often away weeks at a time helping to implement these changes. Also, I had noticed his secretary was very odd acting at a company Christmas Party, and that was the one he said he had the affair with.

We had parties at our house in the summer and John often flirted with the other wives. A house with a pool easily becomes a gathering place for parties in the summertime in Georgia. I liked having people over and encouraged friends to bring friends. Once, after dark, I looked around and noticed John was not in the house. I looked out at the pool and a friend of a friend's wife and John were in the pool together in the dark.

The next day John said they had invited us over to enjoy their jacuzzi on Saturday. I agreed. We went in our bathing suits with our shorts and t-shirts over them and quickly shed the outerwear once we got there. They had a bottle of champagne sitting by the hot tub. When we started to get in, they said, "Oh, take your suits off. We like to be totally comfortable."

I was stunned. The weird thing is I did not want to make a scene. I wanted to appear cool. So, I took my towel, wrapped it around me, and using it for cover, slipped into the pool naked. John immediately got closer to her and her husband came toward me. I panicked. I felt nauseous. I grabbed my towel, wrapped it around me, and ran into the house. John came into the house, with his bathing suit on carrying my suit. I didn't give him a chance to say a word. "I feel nauseous. I am going to puke. I want to go home!" I sobbed. He said for me to get dressed, shrugged his shoulders at the couple, wrapped me in a towel and took me home. The crazy thing is the only thing I felt about it later was that I could have handled it better. I don't have a clue how that could have been accomplished, but I never disliked John or them for that incident. We did not see them socially again, but I didn't feel they had done anything wrong, just something that was not in my comfort zone. Odd.

John was often not where he said he was going to be. I did not check on him as such but when I went by the building where he said he was at a ham radio club meeting, his car was not there.

Many of the group in MM that were at or near my age were in chaotic relationships at home. I guess forty something is the age where things begin to break down in relationships. There were about seven or eight of us who began to go to bars at lunchtime and bars on the way home from work. We sang, we danced, we drank, we partied, our spouses joined us sometimes after work, sometimes not. Most of us worked for a Section Chief who was a participant sometimes and when we had too much beer for lunch, we could call him and he would put us on leave. We would tell him which bar we were at and if something came up that urgently required our attention, he would call us and we could be back in the office in ten or fifteen minutes.

We often finished the evening on Friday nights at an all-night restaurant with breakfast, then we would drive home almost sober. The nice thing is that we were pretty careful to have a designated driver each time we went drinking and never had an accident or got a ticket.

Once a woman in our office, Mildred, complained to our boss that she did not appreciate working in an office with street walkers. My friend Mary and I took offense and posted a note on the bulletin board that we were not street walkers, we charged. I charged a quarter, enough to play a song on the jukebox and she took credit cards (she was a class act after all). For the next week, men from many, many other departments came to read the notice on the bulletin board and stop by our desks and tease us. Our boss' boss called us in, laughed and said, "I know you girls were making fun of Mildred for accusing you of being street walkers, but this has become a disruption to the workforce. You are getting too many visitors. Take the notice down from the bulletin board and stop teasing the men who come in." We sheepishly agreed. It still took several weeks before the parade of men completely stopped.

Mildred did not get the transfer she wanted. Interfacing with her was tense but strangely even some of the oldest fuddy-duddies in the office laughed it off. One of the older ladies, Virginia, had the whole gang over to her house for a party. She loved our craziness. One of the attendees at her party was the blind man who worked the concession stand in the hall outside our office. He got into the spirit of all of our craziness by telling each woman he talked to that he could guess her age by feeling her boobs. We laughed and warned each other to stay out of reach of his hands. Our section chief's wife did not get the message. We looked around and there she was with Roger's hands feeling her boobs. With a group gasp we yelled "Betty!"

"Oh, don't worry" she said "he is just guessing my age. Since he can't see me that is his way of telling how old I am." We all burst out laughing. She turned red and slapped his hands. He laughed and we teased her for years afterward about her gullibility. She became a welcome addition to our group any time she wished to join us.

Once some of us were at a bar after work, sitting at a table drinking (a lot). I was especially inebriated. I was not the designated driver on this occasion. I slipped off of my chair and landed under the table. When I looked up there was gum stuck all over the bottom of the table. I often lay on my back on the grass as a child and looked at clouds and tried to make out images in the clouds. That gift came back to me as I lay there under the table looking at that gum. I found an elephant. I pulled on Mary's skirt, "Come look at the elephant I found in the gum."

She slipped down beside me and not only saw an elephant, but she found an airplane. When we exclaimed over it, all of the other people at the table joined us and we found lots of images in the gum under the table and lay there giggling until the waitress told us we really needed to get up off the floor. We ordered some food and sobered up before going home. That gum escapade was a topic of laughter and joy for many days and years to come.

Our marriages all broke down. We got through it with laughter and friendship and some wild times, not all sane, but healing, as life shattered into little pieces that had to be put together in new patterns.

Chapter 45: The Breakup

Things got worse. One evening John came home from work, packed an overnight suitcase, and said he was through and would be back to get the rest of his things later. I was in shock but not devastated. I knew it was coming. There had been so many clues.

He stayed away that night and called me the next day to come meet him at the house. I went home, angry, but curious.

"I was wrong," he cried. "I really love you. Please take me back."

I was dumbfounded, stunned, disbelieving. He convinced me that it was one of the biggest mistakes of his life and begged me to go to the beach with him for a few days so we could work it out. I felt that if we were ever going to work it out, the beach would be ideal. I am always calmed by walking on the beach. I spent three days walking the beach. We, oddly, did not talk much, but finally agreed that we would work harder at staying together.

Shortly afterward, my job required me to go to Fort Lee, Virginia, for a six-week class. I met George, a wonderful man from Michigan, and we had mad sex every night for the last four weeks of the class. We were both married and our marriages were in trouble, but we were not looking for permanent. We were escaping. The strange thing was, I didn't feel guilty or like I was getting revenge. I just felt pretty and sexy and happy.

At home again, I went back to the old routine. Work, night classes, party, party, party.

John and I went to Bermuda. We were like old friends while there. I felt there was still a distance and it was never going to be any better and decided that maybe that is what all marriages become after twenty years and settled my misgivings with a shrug. Several months after we returned from Bermuda, John was on a six-month assignment to the Atlanta AT&T office. He and three of the other guys from the Macon office had taken an apartment in Atlanta and came home on the weekends. We rarely talked during the day, just at night. But I got a promotion and couldn't wait to tell him about it until that evening, so I called him at work. One of his co-workers who I knew very well, answered the office phone. When I asked to speak to John, he sighed, then said gently. "He is not here. He is on vacation this week." I thanked him for telling me. I knew he was protecting me because he felt John was wrong to do this to me. He asked me was I all right and I assured him I would be fine. I hung up and sat there stunned. It was over. There could be no going back. We were not happy together. It was time to move on.

The next weeks are a blur. I should have been prepared. I felt stupid for feeling lost. I suddenly felt old and useless. I tried to keep a façade of ok-ness. I partied after work louder and longer and cried myself to sleep. My sweet cat, Tinker Bell, snuggled close to me and wiped my tears with her tiny paws. I hoarded my Valium to amass enough to go to sleep forever. I tried to appear normal at work and at play with my friends. I once went into a closet and knew that I could shut down and never come out. I had watched my mother do that and I knew she never fully recovered. The closet was dark and safe, but suddenly I knew I could not let go. I could not allow myself to lose myself. I stood up, picked out some clean clothes and called Mary and we went out. So, insanity was not a way out, but suicide was still on the table.

One day after work, several of us had gone to a bar, laughed, drank, and I felt like this was the night. I believed all of my friends felt I was over the worst of my sadness, so none of them would call me tonight and rescue me before the pills had done their job. So I went home, pulled out my cache of pills, filled my glass with water and had it almost to my mouth when the phone rang. I did not want anyone to come save me. I put down the pills and the glass of water and answered the phone. It was my mother. My mother is the least sympathetic human being I could imagine. My mother never calls me unless she wants something. When I answered the phone, my insensitive mother says "What is wrong?" The whole bizarreness of it being my mother broke down my whole plan. I burst out crying. I don't know what I said to her, but she was there almost immediately with my sweet loving father. I don't know what we talked about. I don't know how long they stayed. My father worked on my washing machine while I cried and cried and cried.

The next day I saw a psychiatrist and he advised me to sign myself into the psych ward at the Warner Robins Hospital. I did so. I called in sick at work and let Mary and mother know where I was. The first day is a total blur. My only memory of it was the woman who was in the room with me followed me everywhere and talked constantly. I complained to a nurse and she looked at me so pityingly that I knew she thought I was delusional, so I shut up and quit trying to be sociable with the poor lady. She still followed me around for a day or two but became bored when I blocked her out.

They medicated me, put me in group therapy and the shrink talked to me twice a day. I was fed, warm and safe, and I didn't have to solve any problems. They also had an art class for therapy. I started a coil pot in red clay. You roll the clay into ropes and then stack them and smooth the clay on the inside of the pot as you go. Perfect mindless activity with a possible goal of producing something lovely. I made the tallest coil pot ever and it is still a thing of beauty in my home. It still gives me peace when I look at it forty years later.

Group therapy was interesting. There was a mixture of males and females in ages from eighteen to fifties. One of the men started coming on to me, flattering me every time I spoke. I kind of liked it, but knew he had problems or he wouldn't be there and I just let him flirt. One day I was talking about enjoying drinking with my friends and he turned on me.

"You had me fooled" he said, "I didn't know you were a floozy. No good woman would ever go to a bar." I busted out laughing. Here I was thinking I was too good for him and he was rejecting me. I started healing.

After the first week, I went to work and came back to the hospital at night. I had group therapy at night and I met with my psychiatrist and went peacefully to sleep. Two nights a week I went to my master's degree classes on base then went back to the hospital.

At the end of the second week, they suggested I spend the weekend at home if I could find someone to stay with me. My daughter, Colleene, agreed to spend Friday and Saturday night with me. She would leave her husband to take care of my grandson "Little Dale" as the doctor wanted to make sure the weekend was as peaceful as possible. Little did he know the disaster that was before me that weekend.

Chapter 46: And I Thought I Was Lost Before

I met Colleene at the house after work on the second Friday of my psychiatric hospital stay. I looked forward to a quiet relaxed weekend with my daughter. We decided to go to Fitzwilly's, a new restaurant and bar that had a band on Friday and Saturday nights. We ordered our food and ate. The food was delicious after hospital food for two weeks. Colleene saw someone at the bar that she knew and asked if it was okay for her to go over and talk to them. Would I be okay? I told her I was enjoying the music and I would be fine. And I was.

After a little while a young man came over and asked could he sit with me. I smiled. He was so young, late twenties at the most, what was he doing with this forty-year-old woman? He started telling me about the beautiful woman who had just broken up with him. She was older than him and he had found her so kind and loving. As he talked, I began to think he looked familiar. I asked him what his name was. He said Tommy Blount. I started laughing. He looked startled and began to get up.

"No, no, sit down." I said, "I am Peggy Barrett, now Burdge. I used to babysit for you when you were a newborn."

He looked at me closely, "Maybe that is why I was so drawn to come over and talk to you. Some part of me knew you were the Peggy who I had my first crush on. You were always so beautiful. And you always took such good care of me until I was too old for a babysitter." As we laughed and recalled incidents from his childhood like the tornado and the time I grabbed him out of the street because a car was coming.

Colleene returned to the table. I introduced her and told her that he was one of the Blount children that I had babysat for.

She sat down and they began to have a conversation about the music. I happily listened to their conversation and the music. After a little while she turned to Tommy and said, "I guess you will have a hard time deciding who you want to sleep with tonight, me or my mother." I was appalled. Tommy got red-faced and jittery. We were in a booth and Colleene sat beside him and he could not get out.

"Let Tommy out of the booth," I said through gritted teeth. She grinned, got up, and waved him out of the booth. She sat down.

"What are you doing?" I said, trying to control my anger and dismay.

"I am having a good time," she said.

"I am going home," I mumbled. "Are you going to come with me?"

"Naw, Mom, I can get a ride home, you just run on along." She nonchalantly smiled a satisfied smile at me.

I left dumbfounded. I tried to wait up for her to come home, but the medications that I was taking for depression and anxiety, kicked in and I went to sleep before she came in.

I woke long before she did and cooked some breakfast. I waited and waited. Finally, I could stand it longer and I woke her up and offered her some pancakes. She laughed and said she would take some coffee. In a little while she came to the table and sat down.

"Colleene, you can't proposition men, they don't like it and they will treat you like cheap trash if you are too easy. Besides, you are married. What were you thinking?" I asked trying to sound reasonable, but really concerned about the girl I had seen in her at Fitzwilly's the night before.

She started laughing. "You are trying to tell me how to act with men. Who do you think you are? I know more about men than you will ever know. John never loved you. He loved me and only stayed with you to be near me. We have been having sex right under your nose and you never even knew it. You can't teach me a thing about men because you don't have a clue."

I sat frozen. She laughed, got up, patted me on the back, and said, "It's all right mama, we can talk about this later. I think I will go back home now." and she packed her bags and left.

I don't remember the rest of the weekend, but I think I checked back in at the hospital that afternoon and they found my psychiatrist and he came and talked to me.

I had two more weeks at the hospital after work on weekdays and all day on the next weekend. We, the doctors and I, decided that I was okay to check out on the second Friday after the disaster of my last weekend out. I went home.

The odd thing is the only thing I felt toward Colleene was guilt. My psychiatrist assured me that the one thing that destroyed my mental health was guilt. How does one get over the guilt of realizing that your daughter has been manipulated by a man that you married and believed you loved? She was not okay as her diatribe at me showed.

My first instinct was to get him put in jail so that he could never do this to another child. My shrink assured me that no jury would ever convict him on evidence given by a wife going through a divorce who had recently spent thirty days in a psych ward of a hospital. I immediately saw the rationality of that. So, I was helpless to stop him doing it in the future. When he called me the next time as he had been doing intermittently since he left, I confronted him with Colleene's confession. He sighed and said, "I wondered how long it would take her to tell you once I was no longer on the scene." I hung up.

I worked, went to night school, partied, started working backstage on plays at the Warner Robins Little Theatre. The oddest thing is that I no longer felt suicidal. I had regular sessions with group therapy and private sessions with my new psychiatrist. My older psych told me he liked me too much and that made him lose perspective, so he asked me to try a new doctor that had just joined his practice. The new doctor did not listen very well to my long stories, somewhere in the middle, he always said, "Just remember, Peggy, you are a very kind person. If you never forget that you will always be okay."

Gradually I began to understand. If I were a truly kind person, then I could not have allowed this to happen to my daughter. The reason I was so easily fooled by John was because I was a genuinely kind person and could not imagine that anyone I knew would be capable of being as awful as John was. Yes, I was naïve, but only because I was kind and did not look for bad things in other people. Was I going to be more wary in the future? Yes! But, my doctor asked, would I want to be the kind of person who never trusted anyone ever again. I had to think about that question for a very long time. I did not like people who never trusted anyone. I did not want to be one that kind of people. So I gradually allowed myself to begin to trust again.

Part V: Learning to Live

Chapter 47: Putting the Pieces Back Together

My world was shattered. Nothing was as it seemed. But I was not alone. It amazes me how many people worked so hard to help me rebuild a life. Two of my former students, Rachelle Barlow and Ken Adkins, worked out a schedule whereby every night one called or came by to make certain I ate and was not alone. It took a while before I even realized that they had worked out a plan. We never talked about me. Rachelle was dating a sweet boy also named Ken (Abney) and he helped me with my class on computers. Ken Adkins brought his guitar and played for me. He also taught me some Thai food dishes. He was in a relationship with a Thai girl at the time and we talked and laughed about life and her unusual view of Americans.

Every Saturday morning I woke to noise from my yard. My sweet dad was tending to my grass and bushes. I would make a pot of coffee and we would sit on the closed-in back porch and just be. My father was a very quiet man and sometimes we did not talk at all. Sometimes he told me stories about his childhood. He learned to swim by being taken out on a boat and thrown into the river and watched his stepfather leave him there. It was not a pitiful tale like he felt he was mistreated. It was just a tale of how different his life was from mine. He told of the joy of knowing where all the beehives were because he and his grandfather spent lots of time in the woods together gathering honey and locust beans to make wine with, and of picking wild plums and blackberries and drying them on the tin roof of a shed. These stories were soothing stories and when he left usually by eight o'clock, I felt like I had taken a walk in a cool garden where it was safe.

Work was a challenge, which was perfect. I had taken the promotion that I had called John about just before disaster struck. It was good that I had a haven of people who did not know my story to report to each day. I had lots of new things to learn. My new job was very similar to my old job in MM except the customers were Air Forces of foreign countries. I made certain that Iran and Israel had support for their F15 fighter jets that the US Air Force had provided them. It was exciting and frustrating. Just the thing I needed to distract me from other problems.

Once I had a problem with my Israeli contact getting very frustrated that he was not receiving his parts on time. My boss set up a trip for me to go to St. Louis to a conference to meet with the Israeli colonel wherein he would be briefed on all of his concerns with the United States Air Force and manufacturers of the airplanes. I had done all of my research on the delays in shipment of the parts going to Israel and had discovered that the bottleneck was at the port in Haifa. I had the people at the port fax my copies of the documents where they had signed for and accepted the parts months before the parts were received at the base where the colonel worked. I knew I could not just tell him we shipped on time. I had to have proof. When I began my briefing, I was laying the groundwork by showing all of the parts that we had shipped and their shipping dates. The colonel angrily stood up and rudely said "Just get the damned parts to me on time."

I looked at him and my schoolteacher persona took over. "Just sit down and hush and I will provide everything you need to know in the order I have prepared." He sat down. When I got to the part where the items were sitting in Haifa, I showed the signed receiving slips after each part that he had been sending me nasty letters about. He was very quiet. I finished my briefing with, "Therefore, as you can see, the problem is not with the United States Air Force, colonel." He huffed and I left the room. My boss met me in the hall. "You told the envoy from the Israeli Air Force to sit down and shut up. What were you thinking?"

"I was thinking that if I tried to explain everything to him it would take all day. If he saw the copies of the signed receipts there would be no argument. Therefore, the only logical thing to do was show him the receipts before I told him that he needed to clean his own house before trying to clean mine." My boss started laughing. "It worked. But it was a gutsy move on your part. You will probably hear more about this when you get home."

I shrugged "I didn't mean to embarrass him. I just knew the fastest way to get through it was show the receipts before I went into the details."

As I was getting ready to leave the conference that afternoon, I was filled with dread when I saw the colonel walking toward me. He smiled and asked me to go out to dinner with him. He was really good looking and I was disappointed that I could not accept his offer, but I had someone waiting for me at the hotel.

When I had talked to my sweet friend, George, who, as you know I had a passionate interlude with in Fort Lee, Virginia, at a USAF school there, he had offered to come spend the week with me. I had accepted. We were in the middle of another passionate interlude and no Israeli colonel could tempt me away from that.

When, after bidding sweet George a fond farewell, I returned to the office on Monday. I was immediately called to the office of the Division Chief. "What were you thinking telling an Israeli colonel to sit down and shut up?" he asked in a tone of voice somewhere between frustration and awe.

"I am sorry. I should have been more respectful. It just sorta came out that way. I knew if he would just give me a few more minutes I would have all of his answers for him. I could have expressed it more politely."

He sputtered. "Just remember that in the future."

I quickly became well known in my new job as a person not to be messed with. I was just fine with that.

Chapter 48: New Outlooks

One Saturday when daddy didn't make it over to work on my yard, I got on the riding lawn mower and began to mow the yard. While mowing I got angrier and angrier that I was forty years old and living alone and had to do all the maintenance on my home, yard, and pool. Poor pitiful me. Waa, Waa, Waa! Then it hit me. I owned this house all by myself. I didn't have to take any more flak from anybody. I could swim when I wanted to. I could go out when I wanted to. I didn't have to consider anyone else when I decided what I wanted for dinner and when I wanted to eat. I could come home from work and have a glass of wine and swim and then have cheese and crackers if I wanted to. I didn't have anyone else I had to please. I was free. I had enough money to do all the things I had not done before, like travel anywhere I wanted to without consulting anyone. I WAS FREE! Suddenly I was happy and began to sing as I cut MY lawn.

One of the things that had happened with my partying with my friends was that sometimes just the girls would go for a girl's night out. One night we went to a bar owned by one of the friends of the guys in our loose little gang from work. Happy hour was especially wild that afternoon. The guy who owned the bar, J.T. decided that when the girls got up to dance, he would have the waitress top off their drinks for free. When we sat down from dancing there was always a full drink at our place at the table. The problem with this strategy was that we lost count of how much we had been drinking and drank much more than we usually allowed ourselves to drink. Pretty soon happy hour was over and we were "Happy." We did not want the night to end, so we decided to go swimming at my house. When we got there, we realized that I was the only one with a bathing suit and my extras were not in enough sizes to fit all. My pool was enclosed by high shrubs and it was getting dark so we decided to go nude.

My memory of that night is blurry, but when we got in the pool, one of the not quite young any more ladies in our group suddenly started laughing, almost hysterically. We all were laughing of course, but this was more. She yelled, "Look at my boobs!" We gathered around her, curious.

"They are standing up on their own" she giggled. "They haven't done that since I was twenty years old. Don't they look fabulous." We all looked at her boobs and then ours and determined that indeed all of our boobs looked fantastically youthful when we were naked and they were supported by the water. We laughed and swam and sobered up and just enjoyed the freedom of our boobs and just being together with just us girls laughing. This group of ladies bonded and still forty years later, those of us that are left, like to get together and remember those crazy times and make new memories.

At work somebody told somebody else about our wild night and rumors floated that some of the guys might have followed us and peeped around the bushes that night, but we just laughed and teased them that they wished they had been able to do so.

As I moved on with my life, I began to date. One of the first relationships was with a recently divorced friend of John Burdge's named Jackson. I think my main attraction to Jackson was that he loved to go canoeing. I had never been canoeing and I found it very relaxing. We would put the canoe in the water at one point and drop a car off at the end point. Every other weekend he had his daughters and kept to them and himself. But on the weekends he did not have the girls, we almost always went "on the river" somewhere.

Most of the time we started early on a Saturday morning, camped overnight on a riverbank, and came home on Sunday afternoon. We packed a camp stove, sleeping bags, tents, etc. He did the cooking. We fished intermittently, and since it was always downstream, we did not have to work very hard. Wildlife like deer and even an occasional fox came to the river to drink and, if we were quiet, did not pay any attention to us. That feeling of being alone in a wilderness was food for my soul.

A couple of times though it got very exciting, or scary, whichever term you wish to call it. Once, after camping overnight, we ate breakfast, packed up, and paddled to a place where a tree had fallen in the water, an ideal fishing spot for schools of bream. I was using one of John's expensive rod and reel sets and threw in the lure close to the fallen tree. When I felt a tug and began to reel in the line, it stuck on something. After several tugs, I turned around to pick up the clippers to cut the line. As I turned the line came free and when I turned back to look at the fish I had caught, there was a cottonmouth moccasin with his mouth open wrapped around my line about one inch from where my hand was. I threw the rod and reel away from me and quickly fed that moccasin my already digested breakfast. John quickly recovered his rod and reel before he began to laugh. Funny, I would have thought I would have been angry with him for laughing, but instead I immediately joined him. We laughed and talked about how well fed that moccasin was with his bacon and egg breakfast.

One three-day weekend we decided to go down the Ocmulgee River to the Okefenokee Swamp in South Georgia. We put the canoe in at a place where the Ocmulgee flows behind Robins Air Force Base and began our trek. We had not gone very far downriver when we came around a wide curve. On our left side was a high clay embankment and on our right was a sandbank. The embankment was about two feet higher than my head and we were slightly under the overhang. I heard a whoofing sound above my head and looked up to see the head and shoulders of an alligator right above me on the overhang. My immediate vision was that, if he decided to come down, he would be right on top of me and I would be in the water with a ten foot alligator. I froze. John looked up, put his finger to his lips to shush me, and quietly rowed away as fast as he could without drawing any attention to us from our large visitor.

You would think that would be enough excitement for one trip, but oh no, it was a very eventful weekend. When we got further south the water was much calmer. Around Robins AFB the water is filled with red clay and is very muddy and a reddish color, as you get away from the clay the water changes to black as the tannin in the tree roots filter it but give it their own dark color. It is amazing how beautiful the clear black water is. It was a very hot day and as we went it got warmer. I had on a bathing suit with a long-sleeved blouse over it to protect me from the sun. As I got hot, I would take off the blouse, dip it in the water, and put it back on wet. It was amazingly refreshing. As we neared the end of our journey, I was about to dip my blouse again. John said very quietly, "I don't think you need to do that right now."

I turned to him questioningly. "You see those eyes right above the water behind us, and all around us?"

I had not noticed them before but when I looked around, I realized there were at least four or five sets of eyes near the canoe. "Yes. Aren't those frog?"

"Well, no, my love, those are alligators and they have been following us for a little while now. They won't be a problem if you don't give them the delicate little morsel of your white hand. So, you will be safe as long as we keep all of our parts in this safe little canoe."

I decided that I really could do without dipping my blouse in the water for a while. We reached shore safely and I stored up the story of my weekend with the alligators to share with any unsuspecting victims of my storytelling in the future. Now you have heard it. Aren't you blessed?

Life was good and new adventures awaited me in my time learning to live in my own little house and my world that I now owned without any obligations to anyone else. And I found so many people that I could share it with and still own my own space and soul.

Chapter 49: The Girls

The initial group of "the girls" grew from our working group in MM. I had met Mary when I still worked in contracts. One of her friends was an engineer who had written the "statement of work" for one of my contracts, and as we rewrote the document with the contractor, he and I had become friends. He surprised me one day when he brought Mary over to meet me, because he said, "I think you and Mary will enjoy each other's company," and I had sort of forgotten the whole incident until I transferred to MM and she occupied the desk right across the aisle from where I sat. We immediately started up the friendship that had not developed after that first meeting.

Then there was the financial person in the office, Virginia. Virginia was the unlikeliest of friends. She was in her sixties, a widow, crippled by a broken ankle that had not healed well, and, frankly, curmudgeonly. If you had an error in any of the financial data you gave her, you were in for a royal tongue lashing. She loved the pranks Mary and I pulled and despised Mildred for her holier than thou attitude towards us. Virginia could not drive. She had a friend she paid to transport her back and forth to work. She "was not going to be obligated to anyone!!!" She lived three blocks from me on a street that I passed on my way to work every day. I told her that any time she needed a ride, I would be glad to take her. She said her son worked on the base and he would take her when her regular ride was not available. And so it stood firmly. One day she said, "Okay, I hate doing this, but my ride is not available to take me home tonight and my son is working late, so if you will be a good girl, I will allow you the privilege of taking me home." I was thrilled. I truly felt that it was a privilege and I was honored.

At closing time, I told her to walk out to the docks right outside the office door and wait for me and I would go get the car. She smiled and said, "Don't dawdle, I don't want to be standing out there all night." I rushed to get my car. Got into my mental state of what I needed to do when I got home and realized I needed to go to the grocery store. I began planning what I needed to get at the store….and drove straight there without even thinking about Virginia again until I was unpacking the groceries at home. "Oh my God." I panicked. "Where is she? What have I done? She will never speak to me again?" I dropped everything and ran to the phone. She answered on the first ring.

"Oh, thank goodness you are okay," I blurted.

"No thanks to you," she said acridly. "What happened to you?"

"I had a brain fart," I said. "I went grocery shopping and I just got home and realized I had forgotten all about you."

"I never heard of a brain fart, but that sounds exactly like what you had to completely forget all about me waiting patiently on the docks… forever."

"Oh, Virginia, how can you ever forgive me? You will never trust me again."

"That's probably true," she said, starting to laugh. "A brain fart."

Then we both laughed 'til we cried. It took months before she let me take her home again and I never ever left her on the docks again. She did tell me that her son left work earlier than he intended to and came and took her home when she called him. I met him several times after that and he always looked at me askance when I talked to him, but he never confronted me about leaving his mother on the docks that day.

Another of the "girls" was Linda. Linda worked on the "Mod Squad" with me and was my go-to person when I had questions regarding the workload. She helped grudgingly, so I rarely bothered her with questions. Over time I realized she had a lot of problems at home and only partied with the whole gang rarely, but she loved planning picnics at lunch time at work. Our lenient supervisor loved these picnics and our lunches, almost monthly, often turned into afternoons off, always on vacation time, for our little gang.

Wanda was the baby of the gang. She was in her twenties, but had gone through a very short marriage after high school and was a free soul. She loved to spend money, but justified it by always hunting a bargain. She had stacks of coupons and if we talked about something we were going shopping for, she would go through her coupons and provide us with them if they matched our shopping list and were not on hers. Virginia loved for Wanda to do her shopping. It was a win-win. Virginia didn't have to stand on her feet to shop and it was always cheaper than when she shopped for herself.

Esther was the only married one of us. Her husband worked near us and both her and her husband, Wayne, were part of the crazy afterwork gang. Esther had her own special charm and craziness. She was the clumsiest human I have ever known, not only when we were drinking, at which time we all avoided sitting too close to her, but everywhere she went. She once told the story of going to the grocery store and reaching up to get a can of 7Up. The can slipped out of her hand and knocked several other cans off the shelf. When they hit the floor, several of them burst open and began spinning around spewing 7Up everywhere. A crowd gathered and the cleanup crew stood there and laughed a while before they started advising people to be careful and not fall. Then they began mopping up. One night we were having margaritas in stemmed glasses at a Mexican Restaurant and the stem broke off of her glass while she was holding it. She decided she would not call the waitress until she finished all of the drink. At a party for Carl, she sat next to the birthday cake. Somehow, she managed to tip the cake into Carl's lap. As "the girls" began to go out, we tried to make certain that Esther sat at the end of the table to minimize the damage.

This is where "the girls" began. We added others outside of our immediate work area. There was Marie, a friend of Mary's. She was a shy, quiet, pretty little thing that somehow enjoyed our wild crowd. There was Rhonda, a friend of Esther's and her husband was a friend of Esther's husband, Wayne. She was the comforter. She came with Esther once, and then was there for the rest of our escapades. She was glue that helped hold us together, always kind, always enjoying the antics of the others.

What a blessing to have the companionship of these wonderful ladies when your life is in crisis. Through the years we have all faced hard times, and have comforted, laughed, and gotten sotted together.

Chapter 50: The Legacy of a Loving Father

For a year or so after the breakup and divorce I saw my father almost every weekend. As we sat and talked on those early morning visits, I came to know a very gentle quiet man who soothed my soul. He listened more than he talked. When he did talk, he talked about people who had helped him grow and the wonderful things they had taught him. Grandparents who never kept more than a week's worth of clothes in the closet and gave the overflow to those in need. Days spent in the woods learning to gather the bounty of wild things to savor later, berries, honey, and wild plums. These were precious lessons in kindness, humility, and joy of living.

After almost a year of his visits, he died suddenly of a heart attack. I was stunned and devastated, but had to take over the planning of the funeral from a mother who was more devastated than I. Somehow having something to do helped keep the loss controllable.

I met a new father on the day of his funeral, one that I had never known before. The mayor and city council were at his funeral. They all came up to me and told me they belonged to the Shriners and how they loved my father because he was such a joy to be with. Part of the Shriner parades always included a clown car. They said my father loved taking care of the clown car and each year he cheerfully planned ways to make the clown car happier and funnier and then did all the work to make it happen as though it were the best thing he got to do all year. The only thing they never understood was that he was invited often to become a Shriner and always gently refused.

Then a black man told me he was called Preacher and asked could he take some of my time to tell me his story. We walked out and sat on the back steps of mother's house and he told me this story. It seems when he was about ten years old, he broke into the body shop that daddy and Mr. Wiley owned and was in the process of stealing some tools to sell when daddy caught him. Daddy sat him down and asked what he wanted the tools for. Thinking that he was about to go to jail, he sassily told daddy he wanted to have some money to spend. He was tired of never being able to buy candy or soda. He said daddy sat there for a moment, then offered him a job. Being only ten years old, he laughed and said "you can't make me work for you, old man." Daddy laughed. "No, but I can pay enough money to buy candy and cokes." Preacher said, "I took him up on that offer and he put me to some hard work sanding cars, and beating out dents, and in general learning everything I needed to know about fixing the body of a wrecked car and earning my own spending money. I learned that earning money was a lot more fulfilling than stealing. When I got to be a teenager and my friends were starting to do drugs, I was too busy fixing cars to mess with that stuff. Your father saved my life. He is the reason I am called Preacher. I try to pass his lesson on to all my community. Work on something that you can be proud of accomplishing and you will be proud of yourself. I will miss him. You need to be proud of him."

I assured him that even though I did not know anything about the kindnesses that my daddy evidently spread wherever he went, that I did know of the kindness he had always shown me, and I was proud of him. With that, Preacher hugged me and waved goodbye as he walked away.

I went back inside and two of my uncles asked me to sit down, they wanted to tell me about my daddy's baseball career. I had never known that my father even played baseball. They assured me he was a fabulous baseball pitcher, the best they had ever seen. It seems the little town of Porterdale, Georgia, had formed an impromptu group that played baseball. Anyone was welcome to join in. The team began to get better and challenged makeup teams from other towns nearby. Because daddy was such a good pitcher, they began to win all of the games they played. The other towns became more competitive and word began to spread of how good those Porterdale boys were. They began to get challenges from farther away and the little local newspapers started covering the games. The Porterdale boys were really enjoying the fame until one of the church ladies got all worked up about that boy that does all that pitching and keeps getting his name in the paper is illegitimate. She started a campaign to get daddy thrown off the team because you "Can't have a bastard representing Porterdale. It is a disgrace."

The ladies all banded together, went to the mayor, talking about honest god-fearing people not wanting a bastard representing the city. The self-righteous people in the town agreed. Daddy was banned from playing with the team any more. The team without him faltered and died. They said when the ladies asked him to leave the team, he just hung his head and walked away.

It was hard to lose my daddy and our Saturday mornings, but I gained a whole new view of who he was and I was so proud that these people had honored him and trusted me enough to tell me those stories that reinforced my belief of how special he was.

He was not gone. When I am stressed, I often go down to the river where we fished when I was young, and talk to him. He always listens and I feel cared for knowing he is still out there watching over me.

Chapter 51: Life Goes on and Gets Better

With daddy gone, therapy became much more important. I still had private sessions with my sweet young doctor who always advised me that "Remember you are a good person," and my group sessions. The group sessions reminded me that I was not alone in the suffering from just living a life that we thought was going okay and then discovering deep dark secrets that tore our world apart.

Some of the people in the group had the dark demons of self-doubt that came from somewhere inside themselves that darkened their view of everything in life. Somehow, for me, that was worse than having real things that had happened to me. I could fight my real losses, their imagined demons danced away and then returned at the moments they least expected them. One of these was a sweet boy of nineteen who I befriended. I invited him over and introduced him to my kind lovely former students, Rachelle and Ken, and we laughed and talked together. He enjoyed their company but was very shy.

We talked on the phone a lot and he told me about writing poems. As a former teacher of creative writing, I asked him to let me read some of his poems. After reading them I thought he would benefit from taking a creative writing class and I thought I would enjoy taking that kind of class also. I found a night class at Macon Junior College and we signed up. I loved that class. He was so shy he eventually began making excuses not to go with me to the classes and I went on without him. Gradually our relationship dwindled to just seeing each other at group therapy. Then he dropped out of group therapy and no longer answered my phone calls. His mother would answer the phone and say he did not wish to talk. I was saddened by his withdrawal but not totally surprised. I could not save him from the demons that had been in his life much longer than I had.

I continued going to the writing classes. One night the teacher, Joanne Floyd, told the class that she was planning a tour of sights in England that related to famous writers and she would like to offer us places on the tour before she advertised it. I had just received my income tax refund. The price of the tour was less than my refund. After class I asked her could I give her a check for the tour. She looked up, shocked, "Now?" she asked.

"Well, I have it now and I really want to go," I said.

She laughed, "By all means, let's get it started then. I will gladly make you first on the list for our adventure in Great Britain." She took my check. I walked on air as I floated out of there.

I got my passport, worked, went to my creative writing classes and loved writing. In high school I had played with writing some poetry and a short story or two, but this was much more intense and all the people in the class were very talented.

The great day arrived. I was packed and so ready to go. All of us fellow travelers climbed on the bus laughing and talking as though we were old friends. On the trip to the Atlanta Airport, I was seated next to a lovely woman that was from Macon. Macon is an old established town that loves its history and the citizens love to establish the history and connections of any new persons they meet. In that tradition my companion started asking questions about my lineage to see if our family trees intersected at any place. Having established that my maiden name was Barrett, she then began to rack her brain for Barrett family lines that she was familiar with. I immediately liked her but did not know how to answer her questions. Finally, I just told the truth. "I don't mean to shock you but I am afraid that I am not truly a Barrett, my father never knew who his father was, he just assumed the last name of his stepfather, so I cannot proclaim any lineage to the Barretts." I quietly informed her.

"Oh, my goodness child, I did not mean to pry. That is just my way of getting acquainted. Please forgive me," she exclaimed.

I assured her that I did not mean to chastise her in any way, that I just did not know how to answer her questions honestly without revealing my lack of knowledge of my lineage. She smiled at me gently and we were best friends for the rest of the trip. At one point in England, we joined up with a group of very rich people from Alabama, and when one of the ladies in that group disparaged me, she pulled me aside and said you could never trust the nouveau riche, they didn't know how to act.

We arrived in England and stayed in the dorms at a University in London. I was roomed with a lovely English teacher from Statesboro, Georgia. We chatted amiably and enjoyed talking and laughing together the rest of the trip.

The University provided our breakfast each morning. Imagine my surprise when I saw that broiled tomato halves, "bubble-and-squeak" a kind of potato-onion and peas hash brown concoction, kippers, and pork and beans were part of foods available on the cafeteria line for breakfast. Being a food experimenter, I had to try it all the first day and left off the kippers, beans and tomatoes after that, but I became a true lover of "bubble and squeak."

The first thing that awed me when we started the tour was how old so many things were. Buildings erected before the discovery of America were still in use. A church had tombs of knights in armor and kings and queens from the Middle Ages. We visited a store that could have been "The Olde Curiosity Shop" of Dickens fame. I had never felt before just how new the USA is. History was all around us everywhere. I felt like I had stepped into a different dimension. At the same time so much literature that I had read came alive as I toured this gorgeous city.

On the third day we could go tour a castle or ride the train to Bath on our own with very precise directions. Four of us decided to go to Bath, myself and 3 female teachers from Middle Georgia College. The train passed through the area where we could view Stonehenge from the train. It was more amazing that I had ever imagined. Upon arrival we had lunch. The other three ladies tried to find a MacDonalds. I was appalled. I convinced them to try a British Tea House. The food was soooo different from my Georgia roots. Tea and scones and ham sandwiches on crusty bread with large slabs of cheese was hearty and filling. We then walked outside to a parade where people were dressed in togas and were prancing to horns tooting. Then we toured the Roman Baths. Baths built by the Romans in 60-70 A.D. and they were still there and still beautiful. After way too short a period it was time to board the train and return to London. Tired but content, we quietly watched the beautiful pastoral and village scenery go by. We stopped at a few villages and picked up new passengers. At one stop a man got on leading a blind man from India who did not speak English, we talked to the man who was leading the blind man and he said he had agreed to help the man get on the train but he had to get off at the next stop, would we be responsible for getting the Indian off in London and getting him to another train station that was only a few blocks from the train station where we would get off. I was flabbergasted when the other women agreed to take on this task. We had no idea where the other train station was and I wasn't sure we even knew how to get back to the college from the train station ourselves. They poo-pooed me and said it would be no problem, so the first gentleman got off the train.

As I had feared, when we got off the train in London, holding on to the dear blind man, we had no idea how to get to the other train station or our dorms. The other women panicked and began to tear up and cry. "Oh, crap," I said, "I will take care of it."

I walked over to an older man on a bench outside the train station and asked him was he familiar with this area of London. He assured me he could help. So first I asked him for directions to the other train station which he gave me in some detail. More complicated than I had expected, so I asked him to repeat it and I repeated it back to him wherein he corrected me once. Once I felt certain that I could find the other train station, I asked him how to get to the University from there. He was taken aback. "Just why do you need to know how to get to the University from there" he asked.

Embarrassed I told him that we had promised to lead this blind man to the other station and then once we dropped him off we were staying at the University and we did not know how to get to the University from there.

He started laughing. "Me Gawd, it is truly the blind leading the blind." He exclaimed. But then, still giggling, he very carefully gave us instructions on how to get from the other train station to the University.

All four of us thanked him profusely, and a lot embarrassed, found our way to the train station with our blind man, and once he was safely entrusted to his friend inside, walked quietly to our rooms for a nap before dinner.

The next day we left London on a bus headed to the Lake District and Scotland to visit more historic places where famous writers had written and lived.

Chapter 52: Onward to Scotland and France

Sadly, leaving London with all of its luscious gardens, history, and architecture, we looked forward to more adventures, we were on our way to Scotland excitedly anticipating all of the places Joanne had carefully mapped out for us on our next lap of the trip. Our first stop was the Lake District, where we felt the peaceful serenity that had inspired Wordsworth, Coleridge, and Beatrix Potter. We stopped at a little rustic inn and had crumpets and clotted cream. Then onward to Haworth Parsonage where the Bronte sisters and brother lived and wrote classics of English literature such as Wuthering Heights by Emily Bronte, Jane Eyre by Charlotte Bronte and Agnes Grey by Anne Bronte. There were samples of little, tiny books they made and wrote in as children. Just being in their home and seeing the surrounding Moors made the scenes in their books come alive. I could see Heathcliff on the Moors and hear the rain pouring as Jayne Eyre was travelling up the long winding muddy road to reach her new job as tutor for the tiny French child.

From the moors we continued on to Edinburgh, Scotland, to explore Scottish writers like Robert "Bobby" Burns, Sir Walter Scott, and Arthur Conan Doyle. We arrived exhausted and checked into The University of Edinburgh. We ate in the university cafeteria where we were all amused to find that the free serve yourself drink dispensers had water, soft drinks, and BEER! Those of us who tried the beer found it delightful and it relaxed us into a happy little group as we found our way to our new sleeping quarters. Then we found another new experience. The bathrooms and showers were CO-ED!!!! Each shower had a door entering into a little space with a bench and some wall hooks and then a step up into a shower with no door. All of the toilets were also in stalls. Some of the ladies were appalled, but I felt all the necessary precautions were there to protect our privacy. Some of the students, however, did leave the bathrooms with only towels wrapped around their bodies and carrying their clothes.

At breakfast the first morning in Scotland, Joanne announced that her husband, Dr. Waldo Floyd, was in a medical conference in Paris and he had arranged with some of his fellow doctors a plan whereby we could add three days in Paris for an additional one hundred and fifty dollars if we so desired. It was unanimous. We would leave in two days and spend three days in Paris. I felt like the whole world had just gotten unimaginably more beautiful. I had always wanted to travel and now a magic genie had added Paris to this amazing trip.

Our first day in Scotland we were entertained in the morning by a Professor reading some of Bobby Burns poetry in the lyrical Gaelic tongue. I could have swooned at the beauty of it. I loved his poem, To a Louse-On Seeing One On A Lady's Bonnet, At Church, and was never quite the same when sitting behind a lady in a hat at church. (I was always quite sure that I saw a tiny louse climbing among the flowers that decorated their bonnets.)

In Edinburgh Castle there was a table of ladies who would do an ancestry search for anyone who believed they had connections to Scotland. Their data went back over a thousand years. Having heard that my mother's father, Chester Capell, had descended from Scotland, I asked them to trace him for me. They stiffened up, sat up straighter, and informed me in no uncertain terms that Capell was not a Scottish name and had never been a Scottish name. I would have liked to ask them what about the name upset them and thereby get a lead to where the name originated, but I decided that in the face of their shock at hearing the name, it would be best to find another venue to do my family tree research. I later found that it was Catalan for "hat or hood" and was a nickname for someone who habitually wore a hat or hood or made hats or hoods. Catalonia was a part of Spain.

That night we had a Scottish Feast with Bagpipes playing, Highland Dancers entertaining us, haggis, and lots and lots of dishes that I never heard of, but were surprisingly good. Considering that haggis is composed of liver, heart, and lungs of a sheep, minced and mixed with suet and oatmeal I was not sure I wanted to try it, but being ever the adventurous food eater, I am so glad I ate it. Believe it or not, I loved it! Just shows, almost any food well prepared can be fabulous.

After visiting pubs, shopping, and resting, we set out the next morning for our next Port of Call in Paris. We boarded a train that went from Kent, England, to Hauts-de-France beneath the English Channel, soooo cool.

We arrived in Paris, exhausted and content to check into our hotel and sleep. The elevator was like the ones you see in old movies. The ornate iron framework was open and was not enclosed by any walls. It was so tiny that only two people could ride on it at a time and the suitcases really made it a crowded ride. So much about Paris, London, and Edinburgh, was like time travelling back to another age and yet so fresh and beautiful. When we got to our rooms the available drinks in the little fridge were sodas and wine. The wine was less expensive than the colas. My sweet friend from the bus to Atlanta had brought her teenage grandson with her and he and I decided to stand on my balcony and people watch. We watched and laughed as a woman with a poodle merely paused as her pet did his business on the sidewalk and then they walked away with their heads held high. Other pedestrians that followed, carefully walked around the pile or seemingly sidestepped it without even looking down, then two gentlemen came walking by animatedly discussing some dire business and stepped into the mess and filled the air with French cuss words that neither the grandson nor I knew the French words but definitely knew the intent. We laughed and they looked up. We quickly slipped back into the room and he laughingly left for his grandmother's room. I went to bed contented to be happily in Paris with people I could laugh with.

The next morning, when I entered the little café in the hotel, a waiter asked if I wanted coffee or tea. Filling silly, I answered "cafay aw layte" please. He smiled broadly and asked me was I from Dallas. That was the summer that the Television show "Dallas" had ended the season with the shooting of J.R. and everyone had the question on their lips "Who shot J.R.?" Still playful, I nodded. He quickly brought me some coffee and croissants with the creamiest butter I have ever tasted. As I savored my crusty flaky croissants and coffee, I noticed him gathering all of the other waiters and pointing to me. Since there were no other customers, they came over to me and asked me to say Café Au Lait again. Which I did with my fake Texas drawl. Then they asked me did I know who shot J.R. I assured them that I truly was sorry but I did not know who shot J.R. They smiled and always hurried to serve me for the next 2 mornings and I continued to order my "cafay aw layte".

On our agenda that morning was attending services at the Basilique Du Sacre Coeur in all of its beautiful splendor in Montmartre at the top of a funicular ride. The view was extraordinary and the service was breathtaking. Whenever I walk into any church, I always feel the reverence of thousands of souls that have worshipped there. Whether the religion is one that I know or not has nothing to do with how sacred I feel the space is. I have never been able to be peaceful enough to meditate, however, I feel such a sense of peace in any sacred space that I must just absorb it for several minutes before my mind begins to function again. It is truly peace beyond understanding.

After the renewal of the service, we walked outside to a street filled with artists. I felt I was going to burst with joy. Me, with my inadequate gift for art but always wanting to create more and better paintings, on a street filled with French artists painting just like all the French artists before them. We wandered among the artists gawping at their fabulous creations and snacking on street foods. Finally, around five o'clock we were famished and decided to go into this little French Café that we later learned was rated three stars by the Michelin Guide. There were only about ten tables and we were the only customers at that early hour. The menu included a very reasonably priced early bird "prix fixe" menu of five courses. We all ordered it with glee. Each course was served in a leisurely fashion and we were gradually a part of a totally full restaurant filled with elegant people chatting amiably in French that we only caught a word that we understood here and there. Our French teacher was too busy enjoying the meal to spend time interpreting for us. After eating the elegantly prepared and presented meal, liberally scattered with matching wines, we floated out on our little cloud of totally satiated bliss to find that outside it was dark and the artists had all gone home. In their place, there were "streetwalkers" proudly parading their wares in slinky evocative clothes.

As we rounded a corner, we noticed that the person on the corner of our street was a man dressed as a woman. I had seen this phenomena on TV and in movies but was amused to see it in real life and smiled broadly at him/her. He/she came up and spoke to me, I smiled and turned to the French teacher in our group and she laughed. "He wants to know if you would like to share this corner with him. He needs a beautiful woman to fill the needs of clients that he cannot satisfy."

We all laughed as did he, and then I thanked him profusely. I don't know how he meant it but it made me feel sexy and beautiful and I was truly grateful. Having been deserted by a perfidious husband who preferred only young bodies, I needed a sweet prostitute in Paris to tell me he found that I would be sexy to him if only his leanings were for women. I walked back to our hotel, filled with good food, peaceful feeling from the sacred church, and the best compliment a forty year old woman could ask for, a chance to be a streetwalker that would drum up more business on the street of a man who dressed like a woman.

The next day we explored. At the Notre Dame Cathedral (which was built over the period from 1163-1345 A.D.) I was again filled with the sense that people had worshipped here for over eight hundred years. The French Gothic Architecture and the expanses of stained-glass windows made me freeze and just stare for many minutes, then I had to just sit and absorb the vastness of this magnificent spiritual place. I prayed and then explored.

After a pleasant lunch in the park, we wandered down the path to the Louvre. As we walked in the door there was a crowd before a tiny painting. As we neared, I began to make out Leonardo da Vinci's "Mona Lisa." I was so surprised to see that it was only 30x21." After the huge scale of his paintings in the Sistine Chapel in Rome, this was tiny. However, once we were close enough to fully see it, we recognized that bigger is not always better.

As we were leaving the Louvre, the group was discussing where to go next and one of our group said that she was going to see the smaller Musee de l'Orangerie that was nearby. The others were going other places but I had not had enough of art yet. I had no idea what art was housed there but I was game for another art fix. Oh, oh, oh, I am so happy I took this little side trip. In the basement of this tiny museum are two oval rooms covered in Monet's Water Lilies. I walked into the first of the two rooms and dropped to the floor in awe. These rooms were donated to the people of France at the end of WWI to bring peace to any soul who viewed them. I have never experienced any art that touched me as that room did. After several minutes of sitting on the floor, I roused myself and sat politely on the benches in the middle of the room for at least another thirty minutes. Finally, I was able to walk up to the paintings and absorb the brush strokes. And slowly, oh so slowly, I finally left the exquisite paintings behind and rejoined the real world outside of that room. That sense of awe has never left me when I see a Monet painting, I am taken back to that first moment in that room.

On our last night in Paris, and the last night of our trip, we all decided to go to an Italian restaurant that Waldo and Joanne said they loved. Our long table filled more than half of the space in this tiny quaint restaurant that felt as though it had been lifted straight from Italy and settled into this little niche in Paris. All of the waiters spoke with Italian accents, the décor was Italian, and wonder of wonders, there was a handsome young man singing songs in Italian, wandering from table to table. When he arrived at our table, I stopped with my fork halfway to my mouth and gaped in wonder at this handsome young man with a voice so beautiful and masculine. I could not take my eyes off of him. He noticed my enraptured state and smiled at me. I looked down, embarrassed, but looked back up quickly. It was as though the rest of the song was sung just to me. I felt foolish, imagining that he could possibly be singing to me. When he walked away to another table, we all cheered and clapped. When he finished singing at the next table, he left the room for a moment and I went back to eating. Then I felt something on my ear. I looked up and he was placing a red rose behind my ear. He bowed to me, and tears began to flow down my cheeks. Again, in this fabulous city, I had been made to feel beautiful. I will always love Paris and the kindness of the gorgeous men I met there. I returned home feeling whole and beautiful.

Chapter 53: A New Me

On returning home after my fabulous trip, I found I had a new view of myself. I no longer felt I needed anyone else to complete me. I could enjoy others and love them but I no longer felt I needed them. This caused me to look differently at all aspects of my life. I buckled down and started taking the classes I needed to finish my master's degree in management. The first class I signed up for when I returned was taught by one of the most arrogant jerks I was ever exposed to in my years of college. It was summertime and the classroom was really warm. The second night of class this dumbbob pulled me aside and asked me how important it was for me was to make an A. I answered that I was accustomed to making A's so that shouldn't be a problem. He patted me on the arm and said, "I guarantee you an A if you wear shorts and sit on the front row during each class. "

I replied that I didn't need his help making an A. I was very capable of making it on my own and I carefully sat at the back of each class fully clad. I WAS WRONG. That was the only C that I ever made in my master's class studies. But I did learn a lesson. When a man makes that kind of offer, drop the class. There are other classes out there.

My other new activity was with the Warner Robins Little Theatre. I tried out for a play and did not get a part, but I began working backstage and I loved it. The people were interesting and more varied than I had ever met before. The first play I worked backstage in had a lead actor who was gay. My job was to clear the stage after each act and set up any props that were needed for the next act. I had an experienced property manager to train me and help me make certain I didn't forget anything. The first act was set up as a man's bedroom in total disarray. In the second act he has cleaned up the room in expectation of visitors.

My trainer refused to pick up any of the underwear on the stage that needed to be cleared. I gladly cleared it but curiously asked her why she was averse to clearing the underwear.

"He's gay and I have no intention of getting AIDS," she replied vehemently.

I shrugged and continued cleaning all the items left by her on the stage. Firstly, the underwear was not dirty. Secondly, his feelings were hurt when she announced this in front of him. I found him to be kind and funny and I would never have done anything to cause him any discomfort. He and I would have great fun in several other shows later as we became great friends.

After working backstage for two shows, I tried out for another part and I got a part as a divorced mother who drank way too much. I loved being on stage. I probably emoted way too much on the drunk parts, but my most memorable moment was one of total panic. In one act I come onstage with a tape recorder and listen to my son telling me he will not be able to make Thanksgiving dinner as we had planned. The tape recorder was dead! I froze. One of the actors who played the part of my uncle wandered out on stage and said, "Oh, I forgot to tell you the battery on that tape recorder is dead. I listened to the message from your son and he can't make it for Thanksgiving dinner." I was able to pick up my lines from there and the audience never knew any difference. And again, I was saved by a magnificent older man who kindly stepped in and saved my day. Because of him and his kindness I went on to be in many other plays at community theatres.

I finished my master's degree classes and went to the campus in Milledgefield for my graduation ceremony. It felt weird to be graduating on a campus that I had never even been on before graduation day. But Mother, Jackson, and I had a fabulous day celebrating my newest achievement, a Master of Science in Management diploma.

Changes were coming to my job life, too. The work I did on the base had always seemed the thing that centered me, but one day a man walked in my office and asked me was I Peggy Burdge. I assured him I was and he asked me would I be interested in interviewing for a job with Northrop. I didn't even hesitate. I kept my cool, however, and asked what he had in mind. He told me that they had several government contracts and their contract person in Warner Robins was leaving and had recommended me as a replacement. I established a date and time for the interview. The job was in Warner Robins but my boss would be in Elk Grove Village, Illinois. I was interviewed by the manager at the Warner Robins facility and then flew to Illinois for the interview with Charlie Austin who was the supervisor for the contracts person in Warner Robins. I was terrified on the flight to O'Hare International Airport outside of Chicago. Upon landing I was assigned a rental car, and was dropped off in the rental lot by bus next to my rental car. It was pouring down rain, and dark. I had memorized the map of how to get to the hotel, but I couldn't figure out how to turn on the windshield wipers. I sat there, near tears, trying to figure out where the stupid thing might be. Then I straightened my shoulders, decided a woman in distress was not me, but needed to be me right now or I would totally lose it, so the next time the bus came by delivering renters to their cars, I flagged down the bus driver and, standing in the soaking rain, I must have looked very pitiful. He graciously came to my car, turned on the wipers, walked me through all the other things I needed to get the car started and out of the parking lot, then made sure I knew where I was going and how to get there. Thank goodness for the kindness of strangers. I left that parking lot, semi-confidently, and muddled my way to the hotel with only a minor panic attack when there was a detour for road repair. The next morning, I arrived to the interview on time, and looking more confident than I felt. The interviews with my potential supervisor and the head of contracting seemed to go well. I left feeling very confident that I had done a good job with the interview. Then I parked my car at the airport, with no tremors, and boldly got onto a plane for home.

The job offer came the next day. It was twenty-five percent more than I was currently making on the base, so I could not refuse and didn't have the knowledge to try to negotiate. I gave them a reporting date of two weeks later and gave notice at my office on the base. I was on a new adventure, with some trepidation, but excited by the new challenge.

Chapter 54: Onward and Upward

I could not believe it when I reported to my new job at the Northrop facility in Warner Robins. I had a window office on the front row of the building, a really prestigious placement. The people welcomed me with open arms and I settled in to begin learning a whole new way of life in the business world. Strangely, I don't remember it as a very hard adjustment. With my new found confidence from my trip abroad and my new much larger salary, the transition seemed to go smoothly. Many of the people that worked there in the front offices were former base employees and we had a lot in common and the ones that did not have a government background respected my knowledge and gave me a lot of independence. Which added to my new found confidence.

This confidence washed over into my life at home. My relationship with Jackson was changing. When we originally started dating, I was a shattered human being with all of my moorings whipped away from me by my ex-husband and then by the knowledge about the sham that my marriage was by my daughter. Jackson gradually began to take charge of my life and as I felt stronger, I began to take control of my life back. His reaction to my newfound strength was to punish me by getting angry, stomping out of the house without telling me what he was angry about and then not calling me for several days to a week. At first, I worried about his temper tantrums and then I began to care less and less about whether he came back or not. After all, I had a great new job that was exciting, plays at the Warner Robins Little Theatre, writing classes, and friends that I partied with. I had a full life whether he was there or not and sometimes when he was gone, I began to think I had more fun without him.

Once, in an interlude when we were "made up," I had invited my brother Robbie and his girlfriend, Mary, over for dinner. As part of the dinner, I had cooked some of the vegetables that John and I had planted in a little garden we had made in my back yard. Robbie kept talking about how good the vegetables were and I proudly told them that the veggies had all come from my little garden in the back yard. Jackson got up from the table and left the house slamming the door as he exited. I chased him down as he got in his car and asked what was wrong. He started his car and began to back up. I grabbed the door handle and said "If you leave like this without telling me what is wrong, don't come back."

He yelled back as he almost pulled me down backing up "Don't worry. I won't be back."

Then he called the next week and acted as though nothing had happened. I told him it was over and hung up. One day I came home from work and he had broken into my house and taken any of his things that were still there. I ignored it. He tried calling several times after that and I always politely told him that it was over. I didn't feel like I needed to explain. The strange thing is after spending more than a year together at least several days and nights a week, I felt more relieved than sad about not having him in my life anymore. I found several more of his things in the house and put them all in a bag and dropped them off at his front door when I knew he would not be at home. His calls became less and less and I never wavered in my determination to keep my distance, but finally, my curiosity overcame my discretion and I asked him what he was so angry about that day. He told me that I said the vegetables were from "my" garden, but he had done most of the work making that garden and I should have said it was our garden. I almost laughed at the triviality of the final straw that separated us, but realized that it was never about the words, it was about losing control of me as I gained more confidence. I thought as the weeks went by that it was resolved.

However, one day at work he called and said he was at my house and he had taken all of my pills that I had kept stashed in case I wanted to commit suicide and that by the time I got there he would be dead and it would be my fault. I knew the pills were there as I had never quite released that safety blanket if everything went unbearably bad again. I panicked. I did not want to find him dead by myself so I asked the receptionist at Northrop to go with me and told her what was happening. She and I had become friends and she gladly went to my house with me. He was lying on the floor of my den and was nonresponsive, although his pulse seemed strong, when Susie and I got there. We called 911 and an ambulance showed up quickly. They loaded him in the ambulance and we followed them to the hospital. They rushed him in and pumped his stomach.

In a little while the doctor came out to talk to me. He said he found no evidence of any pills in his stomach contents, so he did not believe it was a true suicide attempt. However, if I felt that he was truly suicidal, Georgia law required him to be admitted to the psychiatric ward for thirty days for observation. "Do you believe he was truly suicidal?"

I did not, with this new information, believe he was suicidal. I believed that he had faked the whole thing to force me to make up with him and he had scared the bejesus out of me. I lied. "Yes, I believe he was suicidal and it would be beneficial for him to be taken care of and watched over for the next thirty days in the psychiatric ward." I assured the doctor. He agreed and I left Jackson at the hospital without ever speaking to him. The psychiatrist's office called the next week and said Jackson had asked for me to attend some of his therapy sessions so we could work this out together. I told his nurse there was no working this out, they needed to help him adjust to the fact that I was no longer a part of his life.

When I look back at this deed, I strangely have a sense of glee. It sort of started a new motto for my life. I will be kind as long as you don't mess with me. But be very careful if you mess with me, you will not like the consequences. Living up to this motto takes a much stronger woman than the woman I had been for most of my life, but it never required a secret stash of pills in case I could not face life any more.

Chapter 55: Growing Up to be Me

I don't know who this new independent person is, I often thought in the days after shedding Jackson. I was living alone, but I didn't feel alone. I was amazed at how wonderful it felt to make all my decisions based on what I wanted to do. Several men came and went as partners, lovers, friends, confidants. Dear sweet George Sloane, my friend and lover that I had met in Contracting School in Virginia, still talked and cooed with me on the phone. We made several trips to be together. Then he left his wife and came to Georgia, planning to transfer to the base in Warner Robins. I was flattered, but no part of me was ready for someone else to live in my house and be a full-time part of my life. I sent him home to his wife. We continued to talk on the phone for many years and some part of me continued loving him for many years, but I no longer really wanted to be a wife.

I went through several passing relationships and enjoyed them but was amazed how little I wanted a commitment from any of them. Then one day I came back from lunch and Ed Vesely, one of the program managers from Elk Grove Village, was in my office on my phone. As I walked in, he gritted his teeth into the phone and angrily growled "You are a fucking liar, and I will have your job." I was totally shocked by his language and that he was using my phone.

"You can't use my phone to say such awful things!" I said in shocked disbelief.

He took one look at my shocked face and stomped out. I sat there in utter amazement. The strange thing is that Ed was one of the only program managers from Illinois that all of the engineers at our facility respected. I had often seen him take off his suit coat and roll up his sleeves and work with the engineers testing the equipment whereas the other program mangers just yelled at the engineers and told them they needed to solve the problems facing them and to do so immediately. (Those program managers probably had no idea how to test the equipment themselves.) I found the whole incident unsettling and confusing.

On his next trip down, he stopped by my office a couple of times and just made a little small talk. Then one afternoon, Susie, my friendly receptionist, said a group was going to happy hour at Chasen's, a local bar, that afternoon, and would I like to join them. I said sure and as I was leaving from work, Ed was getting into his car which was parked next to mine, and I asked him if he would like to join us. He got all the details and said he might join us.

I went home, changed clothes, and made my way to Chasen's. They had pretty good appetizers and a band playing that night. I was enjoying my evening not really expecting Ed to show up, when suddenly, much later, there he was. He was an amazing dancer and the oddest thing happened when we were dancing (now this could have been because I had had a few cocktails before he showed up) but suddenly it was as though I had been transported back to another time. There was Ed in a green satin suit with high buckled shoes and I was in a white flowing gown under a tree at a picnic in France. It was truly as though I had known him and loved him in another life. I told him about it and we laughed but the feeling that I had known him before persisted.

On his next trip after that he asked if I would meet him for dinner, he had a business deal he wanted to discuss with me. He brought one of the other program managers to the dinner and we discussed a plan whereby he, as an independent contractor, would get a government contract and I would work with him on the contract outside of the hours I worked for Northrop. I agreed to his arrangement, but really believed that he just wanted to know me better and there was little chance of him getting a contract.

We talked more at work and I learned from the engineers at work that Ed had stopped a fiasco for Northrop by proving one of our subcontracts with the company who had the basic contract with the government, had told the government that all of their delays in shipping were the fault of their subcontractor, Northrop. But the truth was, they had issued us a stop work order, because they were not ready for the part we were to provide. All of the engineers talked about Ed almost in reverence when they talked about the miracle he had pulled off. That was the phone call I had overheard.

Meanwhile, I got a part in a musical play, "The Unsinkable Molly Brown." I had a very clear high soprano voice and the sweet young girl who got the lead role of Molly Brown also had a very high soprano voice. I was the only person who tried out that had a voice as high as her voice. They needed at least one voice in the chorus that was as high as hers. There was really no role for a woman in her forties. There were only chorus girls in a bar. I became their madam and had a blast dancing and singing. The only real problem was, I was not a dancer. In all of the dance routines, I would, at some point, go the wrong way. One of the young chorus girls complained to the director that I was messing up all of the dance routines and he told her just to think of me as Lucille Ball. He was right. Every time I messed up one of the dances, the audience loved it. I would not have done it deliberately, but I was so glad the director saw it that way. I loved the play, got lots of applause and never tried out for a musical again. Not every director wants his dance scenes to be comedic.

Ed came to see the play and agreed that it was probably best if I did not try out for musicals again, although he loved the play the way it was with me in it. He had become a regular date when he was in town and I liked him. He loved to dance and fit in with my friends when he joined me in a group setting. I invited him to the cast party when the show was over. I liked that he talked easily with everyone and that he didn't hover by my side at the party. Once I looked over and he was surrounded by all the young college girls who has been in the chorus with me and I was curious about what he was like with young girls, having been sorely disappointed by my ex when I found about his proclivities. So I wandered over to where they were talking and stood back and listened. What I heard was so amazing I still tear up when I think about it. He was telling them how talented and wonderful I was. I wandered back to talk to some other people, flattered and happy.

Ed was married. I did not want to be married and made that plain to him. I saw him when he came to town and enjoyed him. We talked on the phone a lot. But I still dated other men and partied at the drop of a hat. I was in a happy place.

I had been dating a cop, Randy, that I basically trusted because I thought he was too dumb to fool me. Then one night we went to a rundown bar in the middle of nowhere and in walked a woman dressed and coiffed like Dolly Parton. Randy turned to me and said "Why can't you dress like that?" Then I knew. He was way too dumb to appreciate me and that was a fact. That was our last date.

Once Ed called and said he was coming in the next afternoon a little earlier than usual, would it be okay if he cooked me supper at my house. I agreed to leave the house unlocked and looked forward to seeing what he would prepare. When I arrived home the next evening the house smelled wonderful. He had prepared salmon with lemon on the grill and a salad with wine. It was prepared perfectly. We talked, laughed, and went swimming in my pool and as we came into the house I was rattling on, feeling very relaxed, and I used a word he did not know. He asked, "What does that mean?"

I immediately became apologetic. I love doing crossword puzzles and know a lot of words that are not in common usage among my friends and family. It infuriated my mother when I used a word she did not know. I had, for years, tried to censor my language to avoid making anyone feel that I was talking down to them. So, as I stammered my apologies to Ed, he looked confused.

"What are you apologizing for? I just want to know the meaning. I love learning new words."

I explained it as best I could, then we went to the dictionary to make sure. He was impressed. I was more impressed. Wow, appreciation for an aspect of me that I had been carefully hiding for most of my life. How COOL.

He made me proud to be me.

Chapter 56: Other Changes

Meanwhile my family was changing. My relationship with my daughter was fraught with hidden land mines. I had a hard time getting over my guilt feelings for not recognizing what was happening to her. I was still in therapy because of the depression and suicidal thoughts that plagued me. This additional guilt added tons more to that weight. I was so consumed with trying to be "normal" and rational that I failed to notice that my son's marriage was falling apart. My daughter seemed to enjoy my guilt feelings and I felt myself gradually building walls between us to protect my sanity.

I determined to be better at spending more time with my grandchildren. I would invite Fawna and Angela, my son's children, over to spend the night. We would swim and play games and eat and laugh. They loved helping me cook and dressing up in my old clothes. We created games where they were princesses or beauty queens. Once on Valentine's Day, George called and we talked and he asked did my new lover, Ed, send me flowers. I burst into tears and explained that he was married and probably did not know how to send flowers without getting caught. Two hours later, the doorbell rang, and there were a dozen yellow roses from George, who obviously knew how to send me flowers without being caught by his wife. The next day Fawna and Angela, my cute little granddaughters, came over to spend the night. When they saw the roses, they immediately decided that we could play like the Miss America pageant. They dressed up in evening attire and gave speeches, then did their talent contest entries, then dressed in bathing suits and demanded I take pictures of them with the yellow roses. It was such a lovely day of fun. I had the pictures developed and gave them copies and put a few up on my mantel. When Ed came down the next week, he asked where the roses came from. I told him George had called and when I told George that Ed had not sent any flowers on Valentine's Day, he had immediately sent the yellow roses. Ed did not ever forget Valentine's Day again.

I also invited Colleene's son, Little Dale, over for an overnight stay once in a while, but he was an ornery child and I had a hard time bonding with him. Once he had a fork in his hand and was about it put it in an electrical outlet, I shouted for him not to do that. He looked at me, shrugged his shoulders and turned and put the fork in the outlet. It knocked him for a loop. I rushed to him. He did not cry. He pushed me away. Another time he found a small can of grapefruit juice in the refrigerator and brought it to me to open. I told him he wouldn't like it and gave him some orange juice. Later, he came out on the porch with a can opener and opened the grapefruit juice in front of me and took a big swig, which he immediately spit out. He threw the can away and immediately ran out and jumped into the pool. I just felt frustrated. It never occurred to me that he might be mistreated at home. For all that she was and wasn't, it never crossed my mind that my daughter would mistreat her child. I was wrong. She had so many mental problems that I never saw, and that rat of an ex-husband of mine had obviously taught her to hide all her problems from me, and she had learned that lesson well. The only side I ever really saw now was the angry at me side and the passive aggression she used to make me pay for her problems.

I did not know how to deal with her. I felt that all her problems were my fault. I had never noticed what was going on in my home. My children were scarred because I was away at school at night and had left them with a predator. My therapist was trying very hard to break through to me that I was not to blame. I was a naïve and loving person who believed a very skilled liar. That did not make me to blame for his misdeeds. Slowly, oh so slowly, I built walls that made it possible to live my life without constantly being plagued by those feeling of guilt.

One day one of my male friends very hesitantly broke the news to me that my daughter tried to seduce anyone I dated or any male she met in my company. I asked a couple of the guys that were part of my group that I partied with did she approach them, they all laughed, as though with relief, "Oh, yeah. We just put her off. It's no big problem, but we are glad someone told you. We would like it better if you don't include her in our parties." I was totally dumbfounded, but very carefully left her out of any plans where I partied with my friends even though she occasionally wanted to know where we were meeting.

As I got to know Ed better. I had mixed feelings about him meeting my daughter. As we spent more time together, I determined he needed to meet my children. I fretted about how to handle that and finally determined, since he already knew about my therapy and thirty days in the psychiatric ward of the hospital, that he needed to meet my family. I warned him that my daughter would try to seduce him. He looked at me with that look that says you are really crazier than I thought you were. He said, "Come on now, I am a balding forty-five-year-old man who is not exactly handsome. She will not make a pass at me."

I understood his reluctance to believe me, but knew what was ahead of me and him when I invited her over to meet him. The first meeting was friendly and nothing untoward happened then or the next couple of times their paths crossed at my house. I started to relax. Then she came over one afternoon and said she had started taking a math class and was having a problem with some of the assignments and would it be okay if Ed helped her. I put on my bathing suit, went into the pool, and left them working at the dining room table. About fifteen minutes later Ed came out in his bathing suit and joined me.

"That was quick," I said.

He stared at me a long time. "I thought you were a little crazy when you told me she would proposition me," he said.

I started laughing. "I know," I said. "You had that look people get when they are patronizing somebody they think is delusional."

"I didn't believe what I was hearing at first," he said. "Then she made it way too clear for me to misunderstand."

"I am so sorry to have put you in this situation," I said.

"No, no, I am sorry I didn't believe you. This puts my worries about your sanity totally to rest. You have been through some bad shit and it is a miracle, but you are not insane."

"Well, I am glad that is settled. Now let's swim awhile and then we can eat. Did she leave?

"Yeah, she's gone."

We swam and laughed and ate and enjoyed the rest of our day together.

New work, therapy, friends, and the theatre became more important than ever and I was learning to be happy in my life. I loved my children and their children, but I had another life that was fulfilling and exciting and I was learning to have fun and be happy. And it continued to get better.

Chapter 57: Tinker Bell, My Friend

My pet cat, Tinker Bell, had been through it all with me. She became part of my life when my children were in third and fourth grade. She was their pet and when she had kittens, she had bonded so much with my son Frank that she would have it no other way than to have her kittens in his bed. We moved her back to her own bed as soon as the first kitten had been delivered, but with another one partially protruding and carrying the first one in her mouth, she climbed back in his bed. We gave up and let her have them with him close by. As life changed and the children grew up, she became the most independent of cats, after all she was Siamese and queen of the roost. She never needed a lot of petting and you always knew you were special when she deigned to climb into your lap. She was the queen. She still had the one personal distaste. She still attacked my brother, Keith, whenever he came over. Once his footsteps sounded outside the door, unless I grabbed her first, she was on top of the refrigerator by the back door, and the moment he walked by, she jumped, claws out, onto the top of his head. Strange. He learned to check for her carefully before entering.

Mother disliked cats and Tinker Bell always climbed into her lap purring. I really think it was to annoy mother. Mother always shooed her away and once she had been pushed from my mother's lap she would saunter away to another room and not disturb us further.

Now I lived alone except for my exceptional cat. She had never slept with anyone once Frank had gone off to college, but now that I was alone, each night she cuddled up to the back of my legs in my bed each night and kept me warm. And, should I begin to cry during the night, she would wipe the tears away with her paws, as gentle as if I were a baby. Our only real battles were when I went on business trips. When I returned, she would meet me at the door, jump into my lap as soon as I sat down, purr and purr, then get up and walk to her food bowl. It was never empty. She only ate dried cat food and Frank would have made sure that she had enough food every day. But I knew she wanted me to put some new food into the bowl as a penance for leaving her alone for a week or so. I had once boarded her in a pet care facility and that had been a disaster. She wouldn't eat and was sick by the time I returned. So, we worked out a solution whereby Frank and his cute, sweet little daughters, Fawna and Angie, came by each day, put out new food and water. Frank told me that when that went over to feed her, she met them at the door and walked to her food bowl. They gave her new food. She ate, let them pet her, then would disappear to another part of the house. He and the girls would turn on the TV and in a little while she would wander back in and let the girls pet her, play with them, and sleep a little while on their laps. When she woke, she stretched and left them. Once she walked away, they turned off the TV and would go home. My Siamese princess was always in charge of her castle. This method ensured her wellbeing but it did not prevent her from venting her anger at me for leaving her alone once I returned from any overnight trip.

After our initial petting and feeding, I ate, we watched some TV together, I unpacked under her watchful eye, bathed and climbed into bed, petted her some more in the bed and then fell asleep. Then the real penance price began. She would leave the bed, stand near the door and begin caterwauling at the top of her voice just out of my reach. If you have ever heard a Siamese caterwaul, you know how loud and scary it is. It is a sound somewhere between a lion's roar and a screaming baby, piercing and heartbreaking. I would chase her, try to console her. She would hush just out of my reach and when I returned to bed it would begin again. Sometimes I would close the door and she would spend several hours continuing her rampage right outside the closed door. Sometime, hours later, she would tire and I would get a restless sleep, and in the morning when I opened the door, I would climb back in bed and we would go to sleep together. There would be peace with her until the next time I spent a night away from home.

When my boyfriends came over, she was always scarce. Keith still had to watch for her when he walked by the fridge but she did not pay any attention to any of the other people, except mother, when they came to the house. Not unfriendly, just a recluse.

Then Ed came over. As she walked through the room inspecting him from a distance, he called, "Hey, cat. Come here." She walked over to him, climbed onto his chest, and began to purr. I was totally dumbfounded. She had NEVER done that with anyone, not even me. Looking back, I believe that was her seal of approval, and boy was her intuition right on.

My life was so strange. A man I had trusted with my love and my children had been a monster and I could do nothing about it. My therapist had assured me that the courts would not take the word of a woman who had been deserted for a younger wife and who had spent thirty days in a psychiatric ward, that her ex was a dangerous pedophile. My daughter hated me and considered me to be totally unable to ever have a working relationship with a real man. I was trying so hard to figure out how to remake my relationship with her. My father, who was always there on Saturday morning to have a quiet cup of coffee with me, had died.

Tinker Bell got sick. My one absolute comfort had a kidney stone. Within a week, she died. I was inconsolable. I had three emergency sessions with my therapist. He was so kind. He assured me that I was not crazy, it was a cumulation of things for me to deal with and it did not mean that I loved my father or daughter less, I had been comforted by the warmth of my furry companion that was now lost to me and dealing with her death was like dealing with it all alone for the first time. I survived and day by day recovered a semblance of peace. But, to this day, my memories of Tinker Bell bring a smile to my life. She was amazingly special. Nothing has ever taken her place in my heart.

Chapter 59: Ed Becomes More

As we saw each other more and talked to each other more, things got more intense. I expected more and he became jealous of the other guys that I dated. Gradually, I just stopped seeing other men even though he was still married. The strange thing was that I really didn't want to see any other men but I still was not planning to ever marry again. My two strikes in the marriage department had made me love the independence of not being married and my relationship with Ed filled my need of feeling cared about without any infringement on my freedom to make all of my own decisions. So, I was not greatly surprised when I told him I had to come to Illinois to meet with Charlie Austin, my boss, and he said that he could not get away to meet me at the airport.

I boarded the airplane, an L1011, which has five seats across the middle. I was in the center seat and glad I boarded early enough that I did not have to crawl over anyone else to get to the middle of the row. As the plane filled, the seats on each side of me filled with two of the best-looking young men I had ever seen. They must have been in their early twenties. After we were in the air, they began to celebrate with lots of alcoholic beverages. They informed me they were celebrating the fact that they had just gotten contracts to be "Marlboro Men," and they were on their way to Chicago for their first photo shoot. In the early 1980's Marlboro cigarettes selected really ruggedly handsome manly men to be photographed as cowboys and put on the backs of magazines and on billboards. These two Marlboro Men sitting next to me, were in my estimation, the most gorgeous hunks anywhere on the planet. And here they were, buying me drinks to help them celebrate.

I was gaga and absolutely blown away by both their looks and their joy that they were sharing with me. We laughed and celebrated and after landing, as we departed the plane arm in arm headed for the nearest bar, who should we meet, waiting for me, but Edward. He was shocked and bemused. He laughed when I introduced my new friends and he gently disengaged me from their arms, and I waved a fond farewell to my lovely young Marlboro Men. As they walked away, he gave me a very passionate kiss. He escorted me to my rental car after fully assuring himself that I was not too inebriated to drive. From that time forward, he always assured me that he would meet me at the airport and he did. I felt pretty and young and adored.

We saw each other every time he came to Warner Robins on business and our "friends with benefits" relationship was working beautifully for me. Then about three or four months after we began seeing each other, he called and asked was it okay if he came down on a Friday and stayed the weekend. I was shocked, but I did not ask any questions that I truly didn't want to know the answer to.

When he came in late on Friday night we had dinner at my house, swam a little, and, as it was getting late, retired. The next morning, he was very withdrawn and I knew he had something on his mind. I didn't press him. We ate a quiet breakfast, then put a blanket on the ground out by the pool. It was so early that it was still too cool to go swimming. I waited.

"I have something to tell you," he said. Fearing the worst, I just nodded.

"I have left my wife and moved into an apartment. I think it may be a mistake."

I didn't know what to feel about that whole statement. Some part of me wanted him to love me enough to leave his wife. No matter what I had told myself, I still felt some guilt about dating a married man. But, and it was a big BUT, I did not want to be married. And most of all I did not want him to leave his wife for me. If he left his wife, he should be absolutely certain that he no longer wanted to be in that marriage, not because of me, but because he was no longer happy there. And so, I told him he needed to go back home and figure out what was best for him. I did not want him to leave his wife because of me. (Maybe a little bit, but he didn't need to know that. After all, even the best of us have enough ego to want everyone to love us the most.)

So, he packed up that Saturday morning, changed his plane reservations and I drove him to Atlanta to catch a flight to take him back home. I didn't know how I felt about it. But I did know that our relationship was about to change.

On Sunday afternoon he called me. "I cannot believe you sent me back to her but it was the best thing you have ever done. We spent all day yesterday fighting and arguing. I realized beyond a shadow of a doubt that my marriage has been dead for a long time and you only happened because there was a big hole in my life that needed filling. I am not leaving her for you. I am leaving her because I cannot live with her any longer. Thank you."

He was calling me from a pay phone near the apartment. He would get a new phone as soon as he could and then we could talk anytime, anytime at all.

I felt relieved and happy.

On his next visit to Warner Robins, we spent the whole weekend together making memories. One of the memories is especially bizarre. He was in the bathroom, I was in the kitchen cooking, and I felt the urge to break wind. He walked in just as I let go with a loud noise. "What was that?" he asked in his silly teasing manner.

"A frog," I answered with a giggle.

When he went back to Illinois, I received a little package in the interoffice mail. It contained a little tiny wind-up frog. I called Ed on his new phone and we giggled. Not to be outdone in this silliness, I went to Wal-Mart and bought a ten-inch wind-up frog big enough to go into the pool and sent it to him in the interoffice mail. I received a phone call from the security people at the Elk Grove Village plant. My package had been large enough to set off security alerts and they wanted to know why I was sending a large wind-up frog to one of their Program Managers. I was alarmed and a little bit intimidated but ever valiant. I explained that I had kissed a lot of frogs in my time and they had never turned into a prince, but I thought that might have changed with Ed. They laughed and cooed at me and then told me Ed was on the line and had told them he didn't want to explain the significance of the frog, he thought they should call me and have me explain it.

He could not believe the story I had made up. He was curious what I would tell the security people and was flabbergasted at the story I told. But it made him look good and did not give away our little secret story about a fart. Over the years I have shared this story with anyone who will listen and you would not believe how many frogs with crowns I now have in my home, donated by friends who love this story.

I began to really love this fun-loving man who enjoyed my stories and me but I also loved my independence and he seemed content with that.

Chapter 59: Northrop and Plays

It is strange how opinions change. When Ed and I were a secret at Northrop, his supervisors fussed at him because he did not go to the Warner Robins plant often enough. As soon as it became known that he had filed for divorce and was seeing me, they questioned every trip he made to Warner Robins and his visits became more and more curtailed. The engineers at Warner Robins complained that he was not there enough, but it didn't change his supervisors' minds about the frequency of his visits. So, we made other arrangement to see each other.

We agreed that Nashville was halfway to Chicago; a five hour drive for me and an eight hour drive for him. Isn't that halfway? I could leave an hour early on Fridays and arrive in Nashville by nine that evening. He left Elk Grove Village at four o'clock and arrived at the motel in Nashville at midnight. We fell in love with Nashville. Neither of us were country music fans, but the little restaurants in back alleys had really good singers and musicians who were trying to break into the big-time music world. These restaurants were cozy and the singers often sang directly to us. Once it was below freezing outside and there were only two tables of diners in this little café that had a piano player and he sang "Sweet Home Chicago," "Sweet Georgia Brown," and many love songs from the 1920s that I had never heard before. Whenever I hear the song, "You Go to My Head Like Fine Champagne," I always think back to that beautiful special night in Nashville.

Ed wined me and dined me and made me feel rich and beautiful and like I was the most special person in the universe. He made me feel smart, and talented, and like I was the sexiest woman in the world. I luxuriated in the warm glow of his attention. For the first time in my life, I began to believe that I might be talented, smart, and beautiful.

Meanwhile, when Ed was away, I continued to play. I was teaching a friend, Carol Rigsby, how to make clay pots on a wheel. I was writing poems. I was acting in plays. My world was expanding. One of the plays I was in was "The Shadow Box" by Michael Cristofer. It was the story of three cottages on the grounds of a large hospital. The patient in each cottage was dying. It was a very heart moving poignant play about love and loss. My part was fabulous. In the play I was visiting my ex-husband who was gay and was in one of the cottages. When he and I divorced, I had traveled the world and had many romantic exploits. I wore twenty odd pieces of jewelry attached wherever there was room for them. They were tokens of my many exploits. There was a copper bracelet from a doctor in Colorado who claimed it would cure my arthritis and anything else, dozens of diamonds from an architect, etc. Each time I entered on the stage the tinkling of my outrageous attire allowed the audience to laugh off some of the tension built by the angst of the stories of these three people who were facing death. In addition, my character was outrageous but kind and loving. And my sweet truly gay co-star, in a scene where he fainted and collapsed on stage and I sat on the floor and lovingly gathered his head onto my chest, told me later that the scene and the feel of my warm breasts had made him wish for a moment that he were not gay. Wow! I was blown away by this sweet gentleman's comment. I, for a moment, was truly in love with him and his kindness to this over-the-hill forty-three-year-old woman. We bonded.

Meanwhile there was trouble at work. Someone had called the FBI and accused the management at our plant of mischarging government contracts. It was a very convoluted case. There were mishandlings of the charging to the contracts that I had warned the management about, but the government person that issued both contracts had directed the Northrop management to charge that way to keep the pipeline open while they worked on the funding for the contract that had run out of funds. When questioned by the FBI, I had admitted that I knew about the discrepancy but had been assured that the government was aware of the mischarges. Northrop management was not happy with me but definitely could not fire me during the investigation and trial.

Ed and I had spent almost two years making time to see each other and talking on the phone a lot. One night in a discussion by the pool, we were warm and comfortable, and he said "I know you said you never wanted to marry again, but I want to be married. I would love to marry you, but if you are certain you do not want to marry, I think I will begin to try to find someone to marry me. I like being married and I would prefer it to be with you."

My world teetered. I was comfortable with the way things were, but did I want to lose Ed? I began to assess all he had brought into my life: the laughter, the assurance that he respected me and thought me beautiful, talented, and smart. Did I really want to let that slip away because of my lack of trust in any man? Did I trust him to stay the same once I became a sure thing? I let him go home without an answer. In the following week somehow I could only think of the good things he had brought into my life. I had trusted before and been badly burned, but was this different? Was he truly different? I went back to my therapist. His answer was, "Do you really want to be the kind of person that doesn't trust anyone or do you have to take that step into the unknown and become a person who trusts when all the evidence shows that another person is trustworthy?" I thought long and hard. I remembered the people I had known who trusted no one. They were not happy people. Ed made me happy. Ed made me laugh. There was truly only one answer to this conundrum. I had to take a leap of faith and trust one more time.

I would like to say that from that moment I trusted Ed, but that was not the case. He has had to prove himself over and over and over again. After all he chose me, knowing my history, poor Ed.

We started planning a wedding.

Epilogue

In 2024 I turned eighty-three years old. When I was younger, I thought eighty was ancient and never knew anyone who wasn't feeble and losing a lot of their faculties at that age. I don't feel old and feeble. My memory is not as good as it once was. I love the analogy that my file cabinet has collected a lot of beautiful memories and it is not as easy to store new one in that very full cabinet or my computer memory is getting full. Either way I seem to be able to recall most of my favorite childhood and early adult memories, but I may forget your name five minutes after you introduce yourself to me. I'm not having any problem remembering my family and friends just newly introduced people and people I see infrequently and didn't know especially well even then.

My body is not as agile as it once was, but I can still walk three miles easily and five miles with pauses to catch my breath if going uphill. My back gets cranky if I don't get enough exercise. I still love creating new recipes and having people taste them. I love creating new artworks whether paintings, drawings, or clay. I love teaching others how to do anything; art, cooking, trying out new foods at restaurants, or finding live theater or classic movies.

I love reading, exploring new novels, learning about famous people and their lives, curling up with a love story or any story that opens up new thoughts about life and the way other people view it. I keep inspirational books at my bedside and read from them most mornings, seeking to find a deeper understanding of God and the universe and my place in it. And hoping that I can find a better way to be more kind and more aware of others' needs.

Ed and I got married on April 16th, 1988. I love spending time with him whether it be doing word puzzles, watching TV, or walking in the woods. He always, or most always, makes me feel that it is possible to reach for the moon and maybe get there. He supports all my hobbies, occasionally loves a painting I do, almost always enjoys my writings, and never fails to love my experiments in cooking. He helps me watch my weight and sugar and fixes things on the computer and around the house that I find befuddling.

I love my friends that keep me young and alert. They share my fears and successes and make them better and less scary.

I love my grandson Philip who lets me share his life's up and downs and calls me just to talk often enough to make me feel really important in his life.

I love my other grandchildren also, but none of them share as much with me as Philip does. Fawna and Angie have very full lives and I rarely hear from them. I am glad that they have found peace and happiness and I wish them the very best in their lives. My great grandchildren too have very busy lives and I am so very proud of them. Tabitha is beautiful, competent, and very much a person in her own right which makes me so very proud. She and her husband are in the Air Force and love to travel. Christian and Marya, his wife, have built a life on their own and have given me a great-great granddaughter, Eleanor, who is a joy to spend time with.

I have two step-grandchildren that are very important parts of my life. Adam and his three daughters give me the feeling of connecting to children and growing up. Adam is growing intellectually and his tastes are expanding so far and so fast that he is a joy to watch as he blossoms into such a fine father and adult.

Whitney and her husband, Daniel, are so caring and kind and make me feel young and like I am desirable company. Their zest for life is so contagious. It is such a pleasure to have them in my life.

My son Frank is my true love. He is gentle and kind and I never ever doubt that he loves me "to the moon and back." He has a full happy life and I like sharing it with him.

My daughter Colleene is far away mentally and physically and I miss the little girl that was so cute with her little blonde curls.

I love my dear John who has adopted me and calls me mom. I love Carol who has been an important part of my life since she was a teenager and joined my family as Frank's wife and has still stayed a part of my life after her divorce from my son. She makes me proud to be a part of her life and makes me feel like I have contributed to her happiness in many ways. She makes me feel like I am important and have the ability to help people achieve goals they may not always feel are reachable.

I lost my brother, Robbie, and my mother some years ago. My brother Keith has distanced himself from me and mine.

As you can see, I love my life. I love the people in my life. I love the friends who paint with me, share their writings with me, share their lives with me. Friends complete the circle that makes life full of forays into other minds that fill me with awe and inspiration. When I hear anyone tell me stories about their life my life becomes bigger and wider and fuller of meaning.

In my eightieth year, I began writing this tribute to all of those people in my life who keep me young and vital and so alive and wanting to continue living so that I won't miss the next adventure.

Acknowledgements

Writing for me required a community. I had a group of readers that cheered me on. They were there from the beginning. My grandson Philip was the first to tell me I really needed to tell my story. He had moved away when he was young and did not know much family history. As I told him the stories, I started including other people such as my cousins Cathy Jones and Carol Gates, my friends Ann O'Neal, Tracie Jenkins, Mary Cockrell, Mary Martin, Judy Sijersen, my son Frank, my semi-family Carol and John Pagura (who call me mom) and others were added as I asked for help remembering details. My sweet friend from my teaching days, Brenda Littlefield, answered questions about those days when I drew a blank. And then as my stories grew, Ann O'Neal gave me books on how to get published; Harvey Wills (who also now calls me mom) told me about his father getting published and gave me names and addresses of publishers. There was a whole plethora of wonderful people who made this happen and I hope none of them feels slighted if I fail to mention their names.

Of course, this never could have happened without my lovely patient husband Edward. No one could ever have had a better cheerleader, companion, and editor than I did with this sweet guide who was here all the way with me.

About the Author

Peggy Vesely, a former Contract Administrator/Paralegal for the United States Air Force, holds an MS in Management from Georgia College & State University and a BA in Fine Arts from Mercer University. She is a proud graduate of Northside High School and currently resides in Bonaire, Georgia, with her husband, Edward Vesely. Originally from Warner Robins, Georgia, Peggy's journey into writing was inspired by the desire to document family stories for her grandchildren. This endeavor blossomed into her debut book, "All God's Chillun Got Worms."

www.ingramcontent.com/pod-product-compliance
Lightning Source LLC
LaVergne TN
LVHW051624080426
835511LV00016B/2169